Condensed Chronology

Jessica Paige Skyfield

who dis? ποιος είναι αυτός? Qui est hic? ማን ነው ይሄ?

من هذا؟ 這是誰？ यह कौन है?

ISBN: 978-93-95224-80-2

First Edition: 2023
Rs. 200/-

Cyberwit.net
HIG 45 Kaushambi Kunj, Kalindipuram
Allahabad - 211011 (U.P.) India
http://www.cyberwit.net
Tel: +(91) 9415091004
E-mail: info@cyberwit.net

Printed at VCORRE PRESS.

Condensed Chronology:
AKA: One Soul's incomplete count of Chronologic Misery
(full disclosure: perhaps a fair read would be mental illness, but this is a broad term) beginning circa AD 1980, Gregorian.
I would like to be remembered somehow. I think we each have this desire, deep down, to be great, to be remembered after our flesh has melted, our indelible mark left on humanity. I want my participation trophy!! Who am I to even think that what I have to say is important and should be printed, taking resources for my words to find some place out of my head, no longer on scratch paper but something more tangible, cohesive yet still largely purposeless? I am not a philosopher, an angel, a prophet, a saint, nor touched by anything special; but maybe that's OK? Maybe since most of you aren't these things either, perhaps reading my words can resound deeper as a result.
Hubris & ego
(ueber alles), Υβροχή και εγωισμός, **अभिमान और अहंकार**
وغرر كبرياء, ሁሪስ እና ኢጎ, 狂妄自大和自我

If someone just took this inscription, “hubris and self above all” out of context and ran, then lol 101, comedy of errors unlocked and the message is lost, skewed through time, translation, and place. Because everything we experience, see & hear, perceive & believe, is all we collectively say we can know anyway, for ours is a life of epistemology, not ontology. My purpose, though, is to try to make some difference. Words on a page that someone can find solace, camaraderie, escape, or pleasure in. Since my Self is transient and my reach as an individual is small, I'd like to put my words down for longer than I am alive.
In addition, I love these two following large scale art memento concept pieces as a way to leave a mark (not for my sense of self but our human experience). The first is a Voyager type craft shot into deep space with a camera, my skeleton, a solar powered mix of music on loop, and some other Earthly mementos. The second is a metal infinity sculpture drilled into the rock of Earth. I am still learning the importance of High Ground this time around, but I will place it high in the desert in an overhang near some hieroglyphics, as indestructible as possible, so that it may last and last...Mysteries for the future from the past. Because once this muscle in my chest stops, or any myriad of things that befall us does: bacteria, virus, other pathogens, clots and swelling, misplaced this or that, war, violence, accidents, fire, floods, famine, perversion (of anything, even justice), so, really–anything–

We are all Nothingness.
& in time, nothing will exist of me, or any of us, really, except any digital or lasting prints we've made (thanks current ideological cultural iteration of 'metaverse'), until these, too, ultimately fail. Even with imprints made through books or screens, in time these are lost, worn and eroded, tossed aside and forgotten; and like everything, it can get sifted, sorted, refiled, rifled, transferred, translated…time passes...and the meaning is (and likely already was) lost. For how are we to know anything truly beyond our provable vision space and our perception? But I can at least try and get something down to exist after me.

Seers didn't see with their eyes.
Cultural documenters once revealed,
reviled, ostracized for importing a dram of drivel.
entropetic, prophetic dust &...
take it with a grain of salt.

Know that I truly want to have made a difference, helped our kind, although the lack of mythos or credentials in story arc doesn't portend a lasting longevity in (my) message; &, the infinite content etherically around us we lay snugly in our beds means the nanopicoparticle that is this book will likely dance about as forgotten dust in the myriad of tangible meta.

IOI 101: Oh yeah, this one time, these angles, I mean, angels, came and told my virgin Mom that I am the chosen one and so I'm just here representing, bro/dog/homie as the son/sun of the one & only God, the light of the world…when I was born, the stars aligned and these three guys saw this and came and said, we have these gifts, and everyone was like, awesome, yes, everyone loves gifts, which shows how important I am to everyone and my Mythos was born because you got to have faith. Sure, but, the message undoubtedly has gotten skewed over the past few thousand years, and anyway, what's a few thousand years in the grand scheme of things?!

Blah Blah Blah Blah yada yada yada…
Illusion delusion…and we proceed...
seeking Meaning and Meaningfulness.
I was and will always be Nothingness.
From dust to dust, like sands through our hourglasses.
This concept is too strong for my current ego, sense of self, aggrandizing and all,
SO, the pages that follow is part of what I want to leave behind…
& I am a product of (popular) cult-u-are,
And all that came before me,

From here and there, snippets of the human experience through a clouded lens of subjective understanding, my literal & esoteric concept of vision limited by the blinders of conceptual perception and reality. I can thus only tell the story of my cumulative experience, imagination, and imagery, here distilled down in black & white in written English form. And, frighteningly, human culture is growing ever-so-niche that we truly all have very different experiences and relevancies from which to pull and maintain links of understanding: the infinite content making us infinitely content also narrows our sight, our reality, our perception.
Somehow in all this growing infinite splitting & segmenting, we must yet find some common ground of understanding: a telling of human experience without egos or ids, beyond mythos & ethos…
& how best to convey it so people want to hear the message (tone, cadence, fervency, drinking this or that favorite flavor of Kool-Aid, religions, cult-u-ares, languages..infinitely split the differences ad infinitum ...) so: music, obviously, but how else?
All I can know for sure is that I am here now, so let me document.
Whether I am not a typical cult-u-are mendicant for knowledge, I have little crumbs of current American life that pair well with memes and clips of our current popular culture, this being the digital era, and me living with someone who is not a Luddite. Some of life's parts are made greater by snipping things away, videos included. Sometimes words are not enough, hence my desire to have this be some mixed media fantasy-land in some parts, because that would capture the sentiment and my place in culture as I am here now. But this is a black and white book of words only, so use your own creative visualization, and if you hear a song line as you read, it's (likely) intentional.
And in some ways, I feel like I've got this one chance; I will not miss my shot (hear my (rap) culture in this line–thanks Eminem; and, also hear the song parody "No One Remembers you" (instead of "I will..."--thanks Sarah McLaughlin for the song and Devin for the minor, parody version)) as a tongue in cheek sentiment from whence this message comes: a desire to create something meaningful, but knowing that all reality is all nothing. And already how many people in the world right now can hear these songs playing and would also know these references?
Ouch, so miniscule. but I'd like to think that these words are greater than the sum of their parts as written, and there's more to them than I can even ascertain: that beyond my hopes, dreams, and imagination, there is a timelessness or universality contained within these pages. And, in some ways, it's true, if these words go beyond my Self and bring an Other pleasure, wisdom, ideas, a nice bedtime story, in that transfer of information, in the 'if no one hears the tree in the forest fall, does it really

happen?'[of course! (sound waves happen regardless) but in the sense of how much of seeing is believing?]--if I don't even try to write my thoughts and ideas and words somewhere will they have even existed? So I entreat that in this typeset and tree bark even if decayed or lightly incomprehensible, if you read this, please, try and take something lasting. Ugh! So grandiose! I guess because I have gotten something for mine by putting this all on paper, committing it to exist, and I'd like to think this will mean something outside of just that for more than just me. Walk this Way. Right this Way–(thanks, Aerosmith, propagators of pop songs, more crumbs of our collective reality.) Minutia milieu, it's just what we do, if I could put time in a bottle, and oh to spend it with you. & here is my Treatise on (my) Real Life through my Ennui of Entropy.

I have, at times in my life, translated Latin works, read Hebrew Scriptures (in Hebrew), surveyed Nepalis on land use and conservation in their village (in Nepali), lobbied to end plastic bag use in US grocery stores (decades ago), read German political thought during the Bush Jr. era (in German), tried to find justice and equity in the United States (pointless!...), discussed food and water equity with Ghanaians, and generally had a pretty good time learning languages and science, seeing cultures and traditions around the world. But what is this vita unless applied to something...so what is that something and when will it matter!? My soul for it all, here we go again.

Isn't this what Paul/Saul/Qoheleth asked for and sought, too?
How to really be lasting and for what purpose?
Zealotry for Good; but what is good,
goodness or anything we should give a sake to.
& what is a sake but a soul, a stake, or purpose
& we love to waste, for goodness sake,
so get in line & enjoy your time as much as possible.
Maps from the past have sea monsters & lake creatures,
a veritable cryptozoological universe & myths of Archons, QAnon,
other made-up and incomprehensible things.
So let us pretend, then, that it's all in folly,
and what's known is known
and yore is lost as meaningless jolly,
The things unseen, merely Lore.
Afterall, seeing is believing, they say.
So that's all it is, Imagination, dear,
nothing worth sorting, cataloging, collecting, and...
no one remembers you...dodo-dodo-do. Ouch.
"Life, then, is an enigma beyond human ability to solve." *

*Thanks *New American Bible* from Wichita Kansas, c. 1970, that proclaims to present the Dogmatic Constitution of Divine Revelation. F'ing Catholics. This translation is pleasant to me, though, for I feel the way Paul felt, that human life is beyond (my) comprehension. As is wont when one line is taken out of a long work, I believe that Paul went on to preach that this is why trust in a higher power is important.

I have never necessarily subscribed to what, exactly?-surrendering my soul to a higher power? Believing in a power greater than myself that is in charge of all happenings? Since I was never conscribed to or told much about Christian cosmology until I read parts of the Bible in college, which happens to be the same time I was experientially and collegiately learning about cultural anthropology, past and present, around the world and still had the Latin and Greek gods as part of my worldview from reading and hearing about them in high school, it's all (largely) story-telling narrative to me.

Whatever the beliefs, story-arc, and cosmology are, whatever label or name they get, the ideas of ours & mine & yours & his & hers & power & good & bad & us & them & fate...it's like glue that binds us into a cohesive group, adhering to established principles; but also, these stories have been used throughout time insidiously, as divisors, scales, measurements, or tools to, ah, perhaps the phrase is "act holier than thou" or, at the very least, import judgment into the equation of life. Plus, if seeing is believing, I have never seen any of these things you speak of, so do they exist? This is, essentially, the cosmology of my life. So I was always uncomfortable when asked to proclaim allegiance to a higher power during a church service, like I was on the wrong side and I better get right with God or...my unsaved Soul is damned for eternity...yikes! Wait, are you sure you have this authority, even? Now, however, I am largely ultimately glad that I don't follow any doctrine or dogma; that I haven't simply accepted a spoon-fed reality. But what am I missing–?! Ultimate FOMO! (fear of missing out). Faith and/or fate...

Thanks to everything that has shaped me for better or worse.

Melcome to my grandiose Hall of Infinite Mirrors.

Here is some documentation, from me to you–[*who dis?*]. Whatever the concept of I or ego or id or ist or anything and everything that came before and was and could be, what can I do but document the small singularity of what I know, have known, and continue to question.

In my life, though, endless questioning often causes unwanted drama and trouble and I am not sure whether accepting and leaving things well enough alone sometimes may be worth letting the world, or others, life turn on its own(self)...& I see that, especially as any message is warped by time, societal constructs, narrowing of sights, iterations and intentions, governments and firmaments, striving to believe in something, anything, the exact wording is, well, trash/chaff in the wind, blowing infinitely through our literal and figurative reality…so…how best then to convey meaning through/over time without the warp and wear of societal constructivist entropy happening? How accurate is anything we even know!? Here's the scientist in me.

Saul's/Paul's/Qoheleth's/(The/his/that/this–oh the pronoun palaver!) message from the beginning of Ecclesiastes is:

"everything is meaningless"

& it goes on to posit that, even still, isn't trying worth it?!

While (I think) this is the overarching message, this interpretation is mine based on how I read the *New International Version of the Holy Bible*, said 2000 years ago by a once rich but converted zealot for Jesus, written down/documented when exactly?

& it's the Catholic version, the *Dogmatic Constitution of Divine Revelation Bible* version of Ecclesiates that doesn't discuss the meaninglessness of everything but rather states:

"everything is vanity," with vanity defined as: "the supreme degree of futility and emptiness." & lol, now we collectively exist in such a supreme state of vanity for ourselves, our cult-u-are and societies…

I'm not including this Bible babble because of belief but rather to show how the interpretation of even "God's" word can be mutated and changed to convey very different meanings over time in different spaces.

And in our search for meaning,

sifting through the emptiness,

sorting through the futility for grains of recognition…

Meaningless revelatory piles, waving from the ooze for attention.

For better and worse.

For bitter and woes.

Use order of operations to solve this problem:

Too much pressure + speeding up time

/ (divided by) the smallness of self (our individual grainy greedy realities each grasping at straws & breaking camels' backs)

= avalanches of anxiety with a remainder (reminder) of what…

In reading over my words, I realize that I've had problems since puberty understanding humanity: why we're here, why I'm here, the juxtaposing tweeter-totter of meaning and meaninglessness, the balance of intricacies and illusions, the festering fenestrations of our collective sight(s)/site(s). And, hey, by the way, since I am here, I gotta do a LOT. But what I write is masked in English and US culture so how lasting is this snippet, really? And as I've aged, things make less sense, really.

A common theme I've felt my whole life is trying my best but never feeling good enough. Thinking and writing wisely but not acting the part, for I wasn't seeing temperance or fortitude around me, so any realization I had seemed worthless, meaningless. One with the masses. I've never been "comfortable," internally. Externally, I have warmth, food and drink; I am even lucky enough to know love; but, I see that I have never thought of our collective human actions as true, righteous, or even good. But fighting this, or even acknowledging and trying to come to terms with it, is an entire life's work. I've tried to distill down these thoughts & any messages I've gotten…some of them don't even make sense to me…I'll be writing concretely, documenting my reality as I sit and enjoy my time on a beach and then suddenly an interlude in my journal/diary/documented reality about creatures never seen, walls of water crashing down; a synesthesia paradise of realities never known by me, laid out there in my scrawling print…so I just press on, unfazed. But in hindsight, I must ask: from whence do these mysteries come? And what can I actually know? There are the books of Revelation, Songs, and Wisdom, documented by Christians and accepted as fact. And these revered words only carry on one cosmology. Wonders will never cease because our narrow realities mandate unexplainable phenomenon; and even as we search and science, there will always be things unknown, unexplained. I've seen scratches appear from nowhere on flesh. And landline phones call 911 while hung up. So as a trained scientist these unexplainables leave questions that my knowing/seeing/believing self lets slip away into nothingness, no real harm, no foul and I accept what I can see/perceive as reality…

Foggy forgetfulness.
For from whence can't always be answered.
Fated: whatever that means.
And I'm not sure but I am always trying to figure it all out.
Always seeking, *never* succeeding…
I've learned these are "hot sauce" words in our white bread world
& we like gray areas.
But it's true: "always" & "never" are polar-izing
I am a Seeker,
but not *always* and I feel like I don't succeed much, but *never* is harsh.
Except science says: "Define the exact percentage as precisely as possible and prove it, please."
Oh parlay the palaver
carry out the cadaver

& get on with it!
So, without further adieu…

Melcome

to my echo chamber. (Ooh, and it's only my voice.)
I'm having fun, (right now).
And that's what it's all about, right?
Now.
Behold the meaningless rantings of a mad(whoa)man.
Sliding slipping sagging
as time warps and wears
picking up speed on the downhill slide.
Infinite neural networks
these/those/them/there/their/they're sliding glass doors shut
but I can still see back through;

LET ME IN!
It's cold outside.
Scaramouche is fandangoing

and nothing truly

really

matters

at all.*

Hit me where the wind blows
& know that endless questioning is nothing but to beg for sorrow.

**Actually, everything matters/everything's matter and this is just a coping mechanism for reality because everything is so big and I am so little and the forces that exist are so great and I don't feel strong enough.*

But I'm trying.

In Ordinum ist Progress.

(What esoteric concepts!--whose order and progress towards what?!)

Literally all our plundering is in the name of progress.

Of course I moved to the state whose motto is Ad astra per aspera.

To infinity and beyond ad nauseum, blundering through all difficulties.

Vogue

MTV. VH1. VHS.
See me now.
Vanity is our very existence.
And what is vanity from your time or place?
A grave sin?
absolute meaninglessness?
frivolities?
trifles?
the path to beauty, glamour, fame?
ultimate futility and emptiness?
[the ancient Hebrews' meaning, pulled from a Catholic Bible...]
Strike a pose.
Dress-up and (un)fair play.
Dirty Dancing, C&C Music Factory, and MC Hammer
wanton abandon of fun & wild energy
Dancin,' dancin,' dancin,' dancing Machine!
Star Search!
& singing in the car,
illusions of grandeur,
until I was told to stop.
Because it was not good.
"You are not good at singing. It sounds awful.
& you're hurting my ears."
I hope I never slapped you metaphorically in the face like that, my dear.
confidence never again known,
forced humility,
climb out of the rubble and pick up the pieces.
the meaninglessness,
realized in vain.

How ironic that my life battle is doing (unconsciously) the same thing(s) that were done to me (unconsciously) as a child and hurting someone I love as a result. Turning the mirror has only just begun for me. Before that I was always looking away and finding the fault outside of myself. That is easier but of course it's never just black & white, cut & dry. And like it or not, some words grow over time. But please know that there is no blame and there is no anger in my words or processing. I do worry that my apology, too, won't mean enough but I intend to not feel attacked and just listen... ¡remember, Self, that just because you don't agree with it, doesn't mean it isn't a valid perspective!...

The Girl Poem: Part 1

I am a material girl,
Living in a false world
of hopes and dreams
of expectations and falsities.
When really it's just kicks in the face and gut punches,
not pats on the back.
Why can't we just fix reality?
Then we won't be afraid to admit the TRUTH instead of hiding it.

The Girl Poem: Part 2

I am a confused girl
living in a material world
of want and desire.
Hiding my true heart
in the false security
of other aliens to the truth,
Burying it in dirt,
layer after layer,
sentiment sedimentation,
until the TRUTH is a buncha lies.

The Girl Poem: Part 3

I am a desirous girl
living in a confused world
of mixed emotions
of love and hate,
passion and regret,
everything you want lined up before you,
falls into a pit, thrown into the gutter.
Cause the rich get it all.
That is the truth I know and see.

12.5

I am the child who wears the same underwear for days.

I am the child who for strives for excellence,
but when and whether it's achieved or when it isn't…
I have no foundation to lean my frail seeming body upon.

I am the child who longs for attention,
support so I don't drift away from the real world.

I am the child who can put on a facade,
& put up a dark, black veil
to hide every inch of my frail seeming body.

I am the child who seems to have a lot
but there is so much more to be
graced
dumped
put
bestowed
upon me.

My Take

wasting paper, wasting time at the
Four Corners of my Mind.
Am I in a corner of theirs?
Maybe not; but I remember
All the dull lagging days of December.

I'll take what's mine,
To have and to hold,
My stake.
Imagination station.

13

Time to shake,
for the thunder to rumble, roar
in my heart
in my mind
deep in my soul
to disrupt calm
(or what was left of calm).
Then comes the lightning,
hot flashes on my face,
The sky illuminates blue.
mind, body, heart, and soul do the same.
Down and out
and the windows rattle fear.
Fear for what's next.
Fear for the upcoming.
Fear for the future.
Near and dear it holds
LIFE.

****

You were with me only a second in this briefly large scale we call life.
A fleeting moment of your flickering shadow
and the white darkness returned.
Holding a death grip on emotion in our weary souls.
It's a trip we call our own,
but looking back,
you can see where foreign, scuffed footprints reside,
Stealthily encompassing all we've found,
On our journey to learn the questionable known.
Thirsting for the beautiful knowledge we've been deprived,
shying away from the hideous truths we have discovered.
A green door into black eternity
In which your apricot flesh was stained crimson.

14

As the sunlight fades,
my happiness dwindles,
night encompasses my feelings.
A cold, dark, clammy hand snatches away my dreams.
You scream,
“Those were my future!
I was saving those!
You can't have them--
they are MINE!”
And pitifully, defeatedly you whisper,
“That was my happiness.”
It has gone.
Or been stolen.
That cruel, twisting fate face of, what was it? (k)night?
Taking what you once held dear to your heart.
But what heart is left;
it's scar tissue now.
A faint remnant of that awful twilight night
when the lurking, sly demon of gloom seduced you,
that twilight day, that twilight night,
you were but a ragdoll,
susceptible to all elements.
The wind blew and you fell for the last time.

And my friend, who is Catholic, and so values Life, has at times regarded Life as so precious, and the Interpretation of Its Value so Starkly Important that she believed each One mattered; pro-life, no death penalty, for We are NOT to decide. That’s God’s work and We leave it to Him. So at 14 I was convinced that every Life is precious and helped advocate for lack of a choice for women to get an abortion, with myself only to choose one later in Life, after being told by multiple older Women when I was 14 that I would later change my tune. Lol 101. “Ma’am, you ordered Karma on a Silver platter?” Around age 20 she had me be her buffer & yes I would visit a random TN death row inmate so she would not be alone in a room with her long time death row inmate pen pal. I became pen pals with mine and lo! He was released and proclaimed not guilty. She eventually taught in a different prison and began dating one of her students. He was never a death row inmate but can never reenter the US for some legal reason or another… He’s been released from prison. My friend and he married and lived around Puebla, Mexico, planting fruit trees and setting up a human shelter. They had to leave once the cartel killing ramped up and must spend time out of the Schengen zone for a while. Ah, life.

These numbered poems represent the age I was when I wrote them. In reading them again decades later, I am honestly intrigued by their semblance of wisdom and word play that I didn't feel I consciously had access to as a child/teen. & in hindsight, I almost wish my parents had been nosy and read my journals because, whoa, little girl, from where is this lost restlessness emanating?? So in today's colloquialisms, one could say the struggle is real for me. I was struggling at 14 (& earlier) with ennui, feelings of deep hopelessness, and some idea of loss that didn't have a concrete basis from my personal life experience. Karma's Ferris Wheel of Fun(?!) even though I had it pretty easy!

So maybe if I want to espouse a message to take away from this book, it could be something like, keep calm and carry on because, really, I'm OK, actually. Don't forget, I can endorse wisdom without following it, right? Lol 101. Remember to recognize realizations as important and not just keep moving along extempore as life goes on, o blah dee, o blah duh.

Things ebb and flow and time heals wounds and tides will turn, I mean:

"I think -- tide turning -- see, as I remember -- I was raised in the desert, but tides kind of -- it's easy to see a tide turn -- did I say those words?"

So maybe we/you/I can find some humor here (Baby Bush quote c. 2004) & I don't know about not worrying about a thing, or not worrying and just being happy, but things will/can/do turn out all right (maybe not every little thing, but c'mon, we have to stay rooted and tethered in/to reality)...

PSA! #neverforget that too much alcohol is a memory killer; short-term up to 100% and long-term ???! unknown knows…yikes!

I started drinking at age 14. How easy it was to find that drug so young: wow. Alcohol can leave you with a happy heart but all other aspects of life get thrown into the disposal of trying to keep things together while you try to claw crawl out of the meat grinder. As fun as it is: Turnt up is tore up. ¡Self! ¡remember that this time!

& assume I always am asking whether these words capture the modus operandi (the MO)? (Ironic to me that my current state of MO, Misery, Missouri…the state abbreviation code for the great work. Lol 101.)

15

I am safe and warm in my bed of nothing.
I find pleasure in wallowing in my sheets that just strangle me back.
My pillow which once cushioned my head now tries to smother me.
But in my bed of nothingness, I am still safe.
I cannot and will not get out,

for though the sheets are a terror,
the unknown is a jaw that I can never open once inside.
In my sheets of relentless and restless struggle,
I am comfortably suffocating.
Burying my own corpse.

15.5 & 42.5

Years later I find a skeleton of what once was.
The skeleton has pictures of happier times strewn about.
trinkets and tokens, trifles
toils, tumult and tension.

The bone sheath holding a dead spirit,
remnants reborn.

It takes soul
& all I had made for myself
was this collection bones,
memories falling/
stumbling along.

I'm too frail to pick up the pieces & put this whole puzzle back together.
Good god, dog, how many pieces are even here?!

(queue the memes of ppl showing off their puzzles only to have them cast about on the floor into pieces in their moment of triumph.)

I've had my innocence revoked.
It was battered, beaten, and bruised,
I held on to a thread of it,
I do still.
I will hold on for dear life even though those monsters called mankind desire it.
I revoke my status in this world.
As part of your plan,
as part of any plan.
I revoke this title of man(kind).
Because I've learned it's about back-stabbing,
false promises and pain
and they want to take my innocence away.

I go up before the panel.
They evaluate me and declare I'm overreacting.
You don't have my heart, my soul, my feelings or my tears
& you cannot judge me and evaluate to take my innocence away.
I revoke my statue, my belief, my everything.
You are an entity.
You surround me and to get away would be, literally, murder.
So, tell me, how do I deal with it?

This, too, seems prescient. How was I seeing/feeling/imagining this as a teen? I hadn't really known injustice by this point, or had anything occur to make me feel this strongly about these esoteric concepts. Of course, teens think they are the only true knowers of suffering, so maybe I just deserve the teen angst Pulitzer. But now, decades later, this poem mimics my pain and the egregious injustice of my daughter being taken by the family court in Kansas: without regard for truth, a desire to ensure they are doing right by their decision, any notion of welfare or follow-through. Welcome to "justice"...how we are feeling today will determine the next many years of your and your child's life and it will be decided in five minutes because we have a full docket today and no we don't have time to hear what you have to say. Or is it worse and true bribery style injustice was lost on me...or could it yet even be that my meddling awarded me purgatory for, as Meta calls it, "going too fast" to disrupt the order of things read: oil and gas industry). Is life fated and I was accessing some deep pain that I didn't even know existed when I wrote this? And add how did my choices affect this outcome??

18

In my prison, I thought of nature. I unfocused my eyes to a realm beyond and saw then what I will see, what eludes me now. I felt the wind and saw the shadows cast long on the land. Did my eyes fill with tears for what could have been, or what was, rage for the lost? No. Did my eyes fill with tears because of a greater encompassing whole and its destruction, or mine?

It could not be that selfish, right?

It was the calling, the lure of trees still bare, their far-reaching purple branches mixed with the blackish green of yesterday. I look and I can see all of time, except only the present is important.

To live in the now eradicates the others, but never is it bad to dream.

Deplorable and imprisoned now,
but dream for tomorrow,
create a glimmer, a spark.
But will it exist as now?

I have some space again here to write, ex post facto, to search out some context, or something to understand my 18 year old self as I prepare this book as a 42 year old, revisiting old writings as I search for meaning in (my) life. (And how is this different from "(the) meaning of life?" (lol 101, or is it thee? Ah, written English. Is one only questioning based on self and the other for humanity, all based on a preposition?

I still didn't even truly know the wicked ways of mankind at this point. I was but truly a naive little babe, but I already saw somehow in my vision space the thoughts not in italics above. So much so that I had to write it down in my journal from that time and now choose to share with you, dear reader, now.

Hopefully I won't be in any real prison, this poem taking on even greater meaning than I can see now twenty+ years later for some absurd thing, since laws, times, and things change; and while persecution is short, prosecution is long and even though jaywalking WAS a crime, the DA is too busy with other cases and since you don't have money for bail, just enjoy your hour in the rec yard until he's free…

The sentiment in this poem speaks to some egregious injustice as I read back over it 30 years later for the first time (lol 101, time). As I visualize what I see as I read, I see someone's land stolen and them just trying to cope with that…seeking to be OK in the present as they meditate on their surroundings, now forever altered. I do truly enjoy the times in my life where it seems I set about writing something that didn't (doesn't) make exact sense to me but that I felt the need to document.

Looking back in my journals, these non sequitur narratives are infrequent but do happen at times: interludes to the regularly scheduled programming and I don't know where they come. It seems like a sentiment hard for an 18 year old to truly grasp of time and loss that I personally hadn't consciously experienced yet then. Prescient somehow, perhaps, but portending what, and perhaps more importantly, when??!

And keep in mind, too, that this is 1998, before the internet had taken over everything and our entire way of life and what we know as reality not yet shaped by the never stopping incessant streaming of anything we could even imagine at our fingertips. Fantasyland play-time of whatever your heart's desire on queue was not yet any one's reality. I went to the library and used the card catalog to write my Robert Browning essay as a high school senior because while I had a computer, it wasn't hooked up to any pippin' hot stream of my each and every dream. Thus, the machinations of my mindspace didn't include Grand Theft Auto, Tolkien movies, the Marvel Fucking Universe, or any real drama at all. My mindscape and vision space was my own and I'd argue now that the things that shaped us from the outside, compared to the endless arrays now, were few and far between. I'd seen Last of the Mochicans ~8 years prior (still a great movie) so perhaps one could extrapolate from there how I could conceive such a great loss from one's rights being stolen; or concepts of freedom of self and the ability to live without outside influence fought for and lost…

However, I could not have seen, from this vantage point at that time, the juxtaposition of society granting and expanding some human rights while simultaneously being strangled and suffocated by others. The powers plead, "Please, yes, please, distract yourself; and don't forget to please yourself from Babylon's best, the finest fenestrations of your collective wonderment, we'll pump in nostalgias, fantasy, and p*rn ignis fatuus. Buy the unlimited drinks & popcorn & candy / jump off the ledge in VR, will you make it out unscathed?

although shadows are long,
the sun has far to go before the time of driving maniacs home to maniacal self-complacency
only owing their lives to creating the stink of bad air, pink sunsets, pollution and smog.

And a redeemer of something they respect and know of wholly believing and accepting what they are told.

And this does not hurt, blind, beat, batter, or injure its children, its offspring, its perpetuators of the plan,
rather it makes them smile.

So how can we continue to eat our dinners, spoon-fed a film of falsities that tastes like salad-
soylent green with envy for the other

&

when we see our surroundings, how can we interpret the speed with which they whir, are we to whir that way?

This poem, too. I didn't know, yet, really what the true Grind is. The daily hard living of paying for all the shit you have to pay for but it still all seemed so futile, all of what was around me, the what, the why, in intricacies of The Systems just lost on me. Let's just look at insurance: car, home, health, life. Geez, we're far from money for nothing. How about nothing for money. Peace of mind. Ah yes, that costs, too, now. Lol 101. It's my treatise after loving Nietschze and not even knowing how much worse pollution is two decades later, wow. And I swear I remember the earth's population clocking 8 billion then, I really do swear, but supposedly we've just made it there in 2022. #yeeouch! time.

* *

For five seconds I had the semblance that I was doing something Real, something substantial, but really these things aren't real and so much still happens. How can something real happen? How?

15 later

Your door is closed, but so is everyone's else's.
Shut out the truth and let the dark hall grow between you.
The light switch is a hard thing to find when you're groping on a huge wall of nothingness.
The truth is never shed on an impendingly dark situation.
One day you open your door,
& find the foundations of the floor have crumbled away,
you reach out and nothing is there.
Foolishly you step into the well of nothingness.
you're a stone dropped in the galaxy of lost people.
We were afraid to open our doors, and poof!
now we're gone.

In flamed

So pour more on and cast it away,
set alight to sail the ocean evermore,
because it's fun and it's wild and life's dreadfully dreary,
blast out an openness otherwise closed,
packed away into taciturn tedium,

Let's have fun while we struggle.

another round, shirley,
we rousingly shout–
let's erase things more surely!

drugs ready to devour us all–
Now ready on every street's corner.

We're set alight/
paying taxes/
Gleefully cheering
Pour more! Pour more!
In the dumpster fire of our decisions.

Inordinable Time

I found these next three poems with no dates in a box. They are mine, but I have no idea when I wrote them.

Our lives merged together
or it is merging
for a time of I don't know.
Locked on the feel of an infinite time.
Along that forever lasting long road
there are many hills, turns, and paths to take.
Some leave you with nothing,
those are the ones I take.
An item can be priced,
up for the taking,
grabs from other hearts,
sitting on a shelf,
which will be taken
from the everyday grind.
Certainty.
Certainly not yours.

* *

If I can sift the sands of time
in equal distribution though each of my fingers
my life...
will improve.
Self-centered. Self-important.
Clueless.

* *

And I felt a pain.
I think it started in my soul.
Or my heart.
And it was a shatter.
Hmmmmm......It didn't ruffle the outside-
my feathers are still in tact and they are smooth.
I haven't stretched my wings in so long.
I remember that it feels good.
Except, accept, expect
I've only just begun and they are still so sore I don't know if I can do it.
With willpower and strength I will feel and know the ...
& goddamn it, I WISH I COULD STRETCH MY WINGS.
(I'll fly later.)

Mixed (me)dia

merde.

I see a finger painting on poster board of a person,

smeared on the paper crude as cave art,

trapezoid head and fraught mouth,

stamping on flowers angrily while simultaneously watering them.

Me circa decades and decades past/passed.

So that is part of me, my make-up, my thoughts on life,

whether I like it or not…so is seeing urban and rural poverty at home and abroad, customs in nepal and ghana, growing food, commodity markets, monetary systems and construction/destruction/manifestation of too many humans' desires,

Including my own.

Seeing is believing.

But how many of our struggles are in vain? Including my own?

But for all intents and purposes, I am stable.

I hold down and work and do all the things.

It's generalized discomfort with reality at a hiiiiiiiiiiiiiiiiigh level.

Still, it's hard to weave myself in the (k)nit tapestry of our collective (straightjacket).

So, here, put on my reality goggles and buckle your seatbelt.

Reality of/by

Mixed (me)dia.

Und Tag nach Tag nach Tag nach Tag, noch, noch, noch.

y dia después dia, después dia, después dia, aún, aún, aún.

et jour après jour, après jour, après jour, toujours, toujours. toujours.

Merde.

Via con dios.

Til we meet again, please, go with god.

Two thousand zero zero party over—oops--out of time.

March 4, 2000

From my diary, written while I was largely blind, with vision lost in one eye and the other quite bad at the time. Ironically, this would be a good vision time in my life, little did I know, losing my left eye's use entirely after numerous surgeries when I was 23/24. Having no real vision through my eyes at that time is what I'm referring to by "trapped."

Oh the days pass on, and I am trapped. Well, we are all trapped, born into our petty lives, all bent on perpetuating them, creating new life. Constantly growing, increasing, surviving the way no other animals can, in an artificial world of our own creation. As we are hell-bent on discovering new things, we destroy what is around us, our world. Each person is their own microcosm, existing only in certain boundaries, impacting only the little they come in contact with; how to measure this?

Why is money so damned important anyway? It is disgusting. Anything to make a quick buck. It forces people to ignore morals, ignore right and wrong, ignore other ways of existing, for everyone needs money to live. Everyone must participate in the vicious cycle of work spend, work, want, spend, work, want...oh it's ridiculous. This story has been told before but it's just so far removed from our lives now that it doesn't matter. Because the only thing that matters is the immediate, the now.

All must know what it feels like to be a cog in a corrupt machine and not know how to loosen yourself, much less create change. This spark of revolution hard to realize because one's place in life is hard to shake off. It is hard to become powerful if you cannot lift the weights holding you down. Extreme wealth is wrong, murder is wrong. One is punishable by death, what about the other? Who dictates the scales on this?

Quoth the Raven, now & forever more.

& as I have gotten older, these thoughts still ring true for me, for all (?) humans in life. & have gotten worse, one could argue, as the above was written pre cell phone proliferation, pre my own selling of my soul to sammelen und horten the mark of the beast, pre streaming sites for entertainment 24/8, pre the full rise of the Metaverse.

And in 2000, around age 20, I was just reading excerpts from the Bible for the first time, with my college loan heavy liberal arts education. Then & still now, I struggle with the Bible as a work that dictates the thoughts of so many, the waging of wars, the granting of god's goodness…whatever it's been used for throughout time as a tool for humans to push an agenda or whatever Machiavellian scheme we're constructing for power & prestige… regardless, I like the concept of scales I have seen/heard about/think of as a message from the Bible: scales are used of, thought of as tools of measuring, be it money, justice, grandeur, power…there are literal and metaphorical scales…they can prevent your sight if that's all you fixate upon…it is not men that need to even need to concern themselves with these measurements, for it is not our place to judge, weight, or measure, only a higher Power's/Powers': so many scale messages!

& Jesus doesn't abide unfair scales.
Take the scales from your eyes.

I read these thoughts and think, yes, down with all of this judgment by man, our measuring and weighing of things, irrelevant. Take the literal and figurative scales away so you can literally and metaphorically see.

And if all our scales of greatness as we Humans see them are no longer present, who will, then, actually be in Heaven?!
And as I type this all out, I realize/know that one day I will (most likely) be blind, and if/then I am granted an opportunity to import parts of myself into the minds and hearts and ether of others, how the lines are arranged on any page won't matter one good god damned ounce of nothingness, [how?!?! With no sight?!? And howwill I even record my thoughts but wildly scrawled loosely on a ridiculous number of pages!] and yet the idea of spacing and capitals is so important now as I pour out my heart and mind onto the page. This of course begs the question of what is considered important / valued and how to measure what is visually appealing versus conveying a message…what is conceptually tangible in the here and now using a constrained media versus providing innumerable benefits beyond measure through some other means of communication...

And this doesn't even touch upon our own perpetuation of self, our biology begging for the endless replication of self
as we collect things for ourselves, our own, OUR DNA,
all while ignoring the big picture or consequences of our Actions, Perpetuations, Inspirations, Perspirations, Subordinations, Subjugations, Proclamations, Sublimations, Motivations, Degradations
& what can truly be perceived from merely black and white words on a page. LOL 101.

Some personal context if you have made it this far:

I write lol 101 to indicate a double entendre of the simplest ideas of comedy through juxtaposition of our lens for this or that, like, isn't it ironic, dontcha think...one broad idea of the most basic level of comedy as calling out the hypocrisy of those listening in a way that doesn't cause anger; just offensive enough to be funny but not insulting and this is fundamental. And l0l 101 is another layer of funny to me, because it looks like some sort of binary code depending on the font: AI computer code for funny. AI is becoming a really big deal.

I do anticipate being fully blind one day due to eye problems I've had starting maybe @ age 10 and escalating starting @ 14 years old. Over the years, there are many medical hypotheses about what could be wrong from many different fields and specialties and it all simply makes me beyond weary. I used to try and fight and check my decline regularly, but in hindsight I think I see that many doctors have done more harm than good. So at first as I typed these poems out, I was taking the time to be somewhat of an obsessive maniac about how some lines in this work were arranged, or what nouns were capitalized, but Cheese Sauce Christ, *I understand, too, that one day my eyes shall fail, and I too will be cast into darkness. What will I see as I sit without sight?? All of Time and Space stretched out in the blackness? Suck-that-up Buttercup, Motherf*ck! & right now, I'll use my sight to space things how I see them broken up on the page and try & use the fonts and spaces and lines to help get my message across. Which is why, in many ways I want to write all this. One day it will be infinitely more difficult to do any such thing. I have been wanting to tell my story, from the perspective of (how deep am I going down my rabbithole right now?) well, ME: parts of a child of divorcees who never spoke again, seeking harmony and goodness, a state level internet activist who had her daughter legally kidnapped by the same state government she's fighting by lies that her vindictive (towards me, I am not judging his character) father presents in a court of Equity? But don't I just sound so crazy, am I right? & the book can't all be about that without a lot of drama that had/does define me but/and, honestly, by calling forth the name of injustice, I only perpetuate my pain. & I'm sick of such negativity, since when I think about it, I have to remind myself to breathe. the injustice of it all, maddening.*
& the level of subtle details that make it my painful reality are lost in time, hence the references to fate & chance & time & perception...
but then, isn't that my Lot in Life, to never accept injustice well & to always fight it, so serve that b1tch those just rewards on a silver platter, Kansas government, and call it done. & that seems like a decently

interesting story, even if you only make it to the first burrough, right? Seriously, sometimes I wonder what leaving things well enough alone looks like. So/but I was also too intense in all/many things, for my child, I see. She is/was a tender soul and I set hers at disease, (dis)ease...Is that also what happened to me? Some doctors I've seen have said such things; my lack of sight caused by nerves shot to hell, from stimuli/stress of/from what have you. But what do doctors know & the older I grow the more weary I become of their opinions.

small PSA: I wasn't going to "curse" / "cuss" in this book because what if one day a child from school saw it and said, "See, Ms. Skyfield does it?!" all sassy and snooty. By which they have a point, and living by example is crucial, yet it can be quite trying. I see "God's workers" boozing it up so where are the real boundaries anywhere and what's truly important?? So, don't use vulgar tongue as your only means of expression, your message then lost in delivery; but, a well-placed expletive is #supernecessary sometimes. & maybe only I care when this book comes out, and that's enough!--my voice, heard. But I do feel I have a story worth telling. & van Gogh was a deeply troubled man, adults didn't care for him, and not many people cared for his painting during his life. But somehow, over time, his images gained prescience. & if I'm hardcore, at least I still have all my body parts, thank you very much. I am doing great. His struggle one inspiring many unsuccessful artists over their one hundred years of solitude. So this book is not FOR anyone, save perhaps myself; although, again, I write for struggling souls, so take heart, readers, I am trying to put something here for anyone/everyone. & if my child wants to read it, especially if it helps with context, I would love that, though I have other things for her.
& I like spending time with my family (what is the definition/who do you define as Family & what do the titles mean to you/me/us/anyone) & how are you made to feel about them? In this instance, Family is my Dad, Stepmom, and two half brothers...having not seen them for a while and then doing it after five-ish years made me realize how precious "family" time can be. Even if it feels the moments are dragging as they're passing, it's all special. Try to enjoy each moment, at least don't duck it up and miss out because you are sick from drinking from the night before, but / & that's the Blame Game some people play. Here is the long & the short: take the Time; give the Time. It will fill itself with words that make sense because they come from a place of love and not anger or judgment, even if from a hypocrite...&, ¡Self, remember: do not push away your own child because you are jealous or make it a competition! #neverforget #hashbrown

Experience

means nothing outside of shaping you.
But even then, two people can do “x” and each has the opposite experience, so really, what does it all mean? Let's sing to the tune of Billy Joel's “We didn't start the Fire” and get it out of the way:

“UK, Ireland, Western Europe, back again, U.S.A, drugs let's say,
college learning, fly away.
Honduras, coral reefs, Ecuador and burning trees,
Ne-pal, struggle and strife, seeing it all, very nice,
Deutscheland, Ghana, Hong Kong and me-maw/
do the research, feel the burn, meaningless and nothing earned.
big(ger) picture?, sit down, get a job.
politics & USA, fair market, gone away,
no choice, guns in schools, IRS Federals.”

As I grapple with
divisors, advisors, connivers, subsiders/
I'm just trying to get out!
my share, what's fair.

& give me, please, the widest of berths.
I'd like to park this ship and...
famous last words...
the ruin of societies.

The triteness of the “very nice” is intentional. I chose these experiences for myself. I'd like to think I was doing it for a greater purpose of learning and achieving…I was staying in light touch with some of the people I'd met along my journey, but communication has fallen away, perhaps one day to be rekindled, but perhaps simply lost to time…

Dudh Baba is dead. & after decades I finally lost the address for the Ghanaian school. Haiti's been inundated and really is no more. The Sherpas are fine, one lives in Japan, seeking asylum from the Maoists. & I see it really is a matter of scale. Lelep and Tiputini are but dots, lost to progress, here in the US we only hear our woes and can barely contend with those. I feel like I haven't been a very good godmother, sorry, Noa.

& I've even lost touch with my friends, as sad sacks usually just blop around. Processors in overdrive as they blip out in misery.

Autonomy for the ages

I've seen the surface of Mars.
Red soil stripped bare, ready for plundering underneath.
Rich, lifeless, stolen from the lush green.
Destroying deep dark mystery
With machines so strong
yet,
they are just one in the entire technicolor dream.
Aluminum isn't even a precious metal,
but you'd never know that for the destruction,
they are willing to go to get it out.
Soon ready to hold liquid poison to ship across the world.
This commodity fetishism hurts, truly, madly, deeply;
and yet what do I do but buy a lifetime subscription?
for shoes and ships and sealing wax, cabbages and kings.
Read: entitlement, thanks Great Uncle.
Talking Walruses is pretty epic.
They're beaching, these days, too, on the shores,
And doing unthinkable acts.
Metaphorical and literal visions of ownership.
It's not MY backyard, afterall.

(above published in the Verse Virtual, March 2023)

And there is always this...1978 to 2023...cheers to 40+ years!

"Never doubt that a small group of thoughtful, committed citizens can change the world; indeed, it's the only thing that ever has."

OK, yeah, right on! Change/fix the world. YOU can do it!

Said Rosie and that Little Engine, John Henry even.

The quote is Margaret Mead.

& Now!...behold

for popular/current cult-u-are times, let's sub evil and rich for thoughtful and committed.

"Never doubt that a small group of rich, evil citizens can change the world; indeed, it's the only thing that ever has." heart emoji.

lost in translation.

What isn't lost in translation? In plays on words and tongues in cheeks?

Was is nicht verschwindet in ubersetzung? Mit Spiel an Wordungen und Zunga in Wangen?
Was geht bei der Übersetzung nicht verloren? In Wortspielen und Augenzwinkern?

अनुवादमा के हराएको छैन? **शब्द र गाला मा जिब्रो को नाटक मा**?
Anuvādamā kē harā'ēkō chaina? Śabda ra gālā mā jibrō kō nāṭaka mā?

¿Qué no se pierde en la traducción? ¿En juegos de palabras y lenguas en las mejillas?

Co nie ginie w tłumaczeniu? W grach słów i języków w policzkach?

በትርጉም ውስጥ የማይጠፋው ምንድን ነው? በቃላት እና በጉንጮዎች ላይ በጨዋታዎች ውስጥ?

अनुवाद में क्या खोया नहीं है? **गालों में शब्दों और जीभों पर नाटकों में**?

અનુવાદમાં શું ખોવાઈ ગયું નથી? ગાલમાં શબ્દો અને જીભ પર નાટકોમાં?

भाषांतरात काय हरवले नाही? शब्दांवरच्या नाटकात आणि गालावर जीभ?

Что не теряется при переводе? В играх слов и язычков в щеках?

மொழிபெயர்ப்பில் எதை இழக்கவில்லை? கன்னங்களில் வார்த்தைகள் மற்றும் நாக்குகளில் நாடகங்களில்?

Qu'est-ce qui ne se perd pas dans la traduction ? Dans les jeux de mots et les langues dans les joues ?

Have any of what we save and cherish been attempts at humor?
Inquiring minds NEED to know.

Besides ILS and SIS*, said the King of Ist through Me (lol 101), I dedicate this to T.S. Eliot, a great poet. No offense many Times Great Uncle Lewis Carroll (facts) or more recents like Geisel, cummings, Montale, Kurmanyaka.

*Isabel Lillian Skyfield and Sideras Isa Skyfield

The Devil and Commodification of All Things

That's the white man coming.
Fight them; do not let their boats touch shore.
For they take and they take.
Then they squeeze some more.
How and when did we become "Other?"
A telegraph from the future: "don't feed them!"
But instead, a rousing call was made–Huzzah!--celebrating a win for seeping, seething colonialism.

"What land is your land, that becomes my land,
From the Redwood Forest to the Gulf Stream Island/
this land was made just for me."

sadly things would have gone a lot differently if more natives had guns.
globalization is progress and order.
so let's each proceed to take & take & take/
our share, our turn, our rights, (YOLO!)/
til we're all left with nothing.
Whose was it?
& who is that [da faq] anyways?

I paid for it; it's mine now.
My this, my that,
This land is my land, from the New York Islands to the Redwood Forests,
This land was made just for me.
Revisionist History hums a tune & we're not monsters,
just taking what's fair, is all.
And what's fair is me with a lot. Lots & Lots and & Lots.

We polarize ourselves just by existing.
& as we want too much,
we are wonting in any true hallmarks of human achievement
outside of ourselves for anything greater,
Save, perhaps, our 50% hybrids or maybe our mates…
as we plod and plunder/
Making space for ourselves all over the place.

Rough Notes on Reality; Lost to the Ether

If voting as a collective action is so powerful and something we all believe is a way to enact change, we must ask ourselves what each and every (collective) action that we all take multiplies into as we live our day to day lives. We must consider what this cumulative DAILY multiplication factor is and act intelligently. The power of our vote is typically a biannual or even quadrennial choice but the DAILY choices in our daily lives cannot be underestimated to create change. lol 101: #lifework #hashbrown #whatdifferencedoesitmake #citizenchange #voteordie

Today we rallied around many different ideas and issues, but the overarching principle for which we rally is a death of democracy. I counter that our democracy is not dead, although we have let it get quite infirm.Now it is all of our jobs to rehabilitate our democracy, to shift the balance of power back to the people. This idea isn't new, I'm certainly not the only one saying this at this exact moment somewhere else in the world. A true democracy is led by the people, for the people, by each according to their ability, to each according to their need. We must tap into that current of truth in principle that this idea contains and apply it to our actions, in our hearts, and with our minds. Our democracy isn't dead yet, and if it truly dies, if this experiment does indeed perish due to lack of a strong popular voice and will of the people, then we are all complicit in that death. To that end, find your voice and use it. Stand up for what is right, for justice. We are all in this together so we better figure out how to work hard and work together to ensure our democracy's death isn't our true reality.

Right before I wrote this, I had read an account of an Egyptian's perspective on their country's attempt at a revolution, largely using Facebook as a way to rally, to express their concerns & thoughts…the novel ability to actually express themselves translating into a collective overthrow, using a common platform to all to (try to) enable democracy. The Arab Spring was not something the world was prepared to accept. So true & real, yet ultimately, ignored. Placed on the ultimate world chopping block of the same infrastructure that made it, to be parsed, diluted & filtered. The US saw this and thought, oh, no, we will orchestrate our own democrazy from within, all of our own volition and contrition. Queue the Metaverse: imagined reality, orchestrated programming, just sit back and enjoy. So I see US as stymied right now, thinking we're making a difference as we accept our purple hearts for being keyboard warriors of righteousness as we do less & less & less...

Trying...

"The Kansas Corporation Commission is able to argue that *not following the Safe Drinking Water Act and EPA Federal Regulations is permissible*, that following their own regulations (82-3-135a et seq.) isn't necessary, and that all public comment, outcry, and legal investigation means NOTHING to an *executively appointed quasi-judicial agency* that controls all oil and gas in our state. It seems likely that all 2,000 improperly permitted hydraulic fracturing disposal wells in our state will continue to operate without abatement."

"Of the 2,000 wastewater disposal wells that the Kansas Corporation Commission (KCC) permitted, OVER HALF improperly followed the state regulation regarding the public notification period."

Our voices were not given a chance, even, to be heard. But no one in power likes questions. The KCC's stated mission is "to serve the people of Kansas by regulating the State's energy infrastructure, oil and gas production, and commercial trucking to ensure public safety." And yet the public, while able to attend the public portion of the KCC meetings, may not speak. To to be granted a speaking opportunity is to submit a request for a hearing before the Commission: the general public is never allowed an audience. All documents for the docket are submitted in advance to the KCC and expert witnesses on water quality, seismicity, or public health must prove imminent harm. Despite the health warning language contained in the Regulations, the burden of proof rests not on the requester of the permit but the people it could harm.

WE the People now have MANY questions: How many more wells were improperly noticed? Why didn't the KCC notice this discrepancy? What other regulations have been improperly followed by the oil and gas industry and/or enforced by the KCC? When will these wells be shut down since they have not properly followed regulatory procedure to allow the public's voice be heard? Even with Kansas Open Records Act, there is no way for the public to look up whether an oil and gas operator's license is expired. Quail Oil's expired in February 2017. Where is proof they renewed to operate the Morris County well that #FlintHillsStewards fought so hard?

The facts aren't important. They're minutia, lost forever in the crushing grind of gears...

Docket 18-CONS-3206-CUIC is one of the improperly noticed wells in Docket 18-CONS-3224-CINV, We the Protestants should be granted a hearing in this docket, invoking K.A.R. 82-3-122. The public at large requests compliance by the Kansas Corporation Commission with their Regulation, K.A.R. 82-3-135a(e), and when wells come before the Commission that have knowingly violated this K.A.R. 82-3-135a(e), they be brought to hearing. Hoehn Oil's application does not adequately follow K.A.R. 82-3-103 et seq and 82-3-104 by not completely filling out their application, leaving depth of bottom of formation fields and/or deepest usable water fields blank or without a number.

I hereby protest BOTH of RJM Company's applications for permits to authorize the injection of saltwater into the Lansing-Kansas City formation at the Riedl Lease and Well No 1 2640 FSL 330 FEL; located in Sec.10, Twp.17S R.14W, Barton County, Kansas and into the Lansing - Kansas City formation at the Doll Lease Well No. 3 330 FSL 1860 FWL; located in the SW/4 of the Sec.27 Twp.18S R.11W, Barton County, Kansas, both with a maximum operating pressure of 1500 psig, and a maximum injection rate of 7500 bbls per day. I hereby request a hearing in this matter before the Commission. I consent to electronic service of all documents in the docket be sent to me via email at fieldsky@gmail.com.

I appreciate the Kansas Corporation Commission's mission to "serve the people of Kansas by regulating the State's energy infrastructure, oil and gas production, and commercial trucking to ensure public safety" and I request as a person of Kansas that the commission places the due diligence for proving lack of imminent and irreversible harm to our infrastructure, natural resources, and public health on to the requester for said UIC well permits. It would be counter to your mission, for the KCC to approve this, or any other UIC well application permit until safeguards are in place that protect the citizens of Kansas from the known issues posed by these injection wells to water quality and quantity and induced seismicity or until the over 21,000 unplugged wells in our State are addressed.

The Doll Lease is approximately 5 miles from Cheyenne Bottoms and within one mile of people's water wells. The Riedl well is also within one mile of people's water wells. (Kansas Geological Survey Oil and Gas maps.) As a citizen of Kansas, I value the international importance of the largest inland marsh in the United States, the Cheyenne Bottoms wildlife refuge, where 148 bird species can be found. Nearby creeks and rivers feed the wetland, circulating water widely throughout the area. In the Spring, 600,000 birds migrate through the area and 200,000 in Fall. Nationally endangered and threatened species are present, including the Bald Eagle, Peregrine Falcon, Whooping Crane, Least Tern, and Piping Plover. Ninety percent of the continent's populations of Wilson's Phalarope, Long-billed Dowitcher, White-rumped Sandpiper, Baird's Sandpiper, and Stilt Sandpiper are found in Cheyenne Bottoms. I request information on where RJM Co. will obtain the 472,500 gallons of water they will be injecting each day. Nearby Wet Walnut Creek is severely degraded per the USDA and both it and the Arkansas River feed the wetlands and water should not be removed from them. I categorically reject Kansas ground or surface water be used for EOR or Class II UIC injection wells.

It was all for naught.

This is my backyard...You want to go to war!?

It falls on deaf ears,
I'm stopped for going to fast,
the fortress cannot be breached.
Time is on no one's side.
Justice is blind,
gagged, stuffed in a dark, dank basement,
and tortured regularly,
f*cked wantonly in her neck hole by depraved dolphins in suits
by progress, by industry, buy-outs &
It was all for naught. It was all for naught.

So I set fire to everything and left it all;
your lines and boundaries don't define my reality.
And I decided to play your game,
dollar dollar bill, ya'll.
My soul corrupted,
and yet my bank account still pennies for a pauper,
but I am alive.

(Rest In Peace Brennan Beyer,
your name lost with time,
an unproven casualty, causality of combat
fighting the good fight
meaningless
but the palpable, tangible loss
can't be proven,
you can't take what you can't see.
you, I, we're but tiny drips, minuscule drops
in the stalactites of power).

I still drink the same water.

In the excerpt above, I pulled out some verbiage of the myriad of formal complaints I wrote to the Kansas Corporation Commission, largely to show that each application for any kind of well (active drilling, disposal, water extraction) was not only its own complaint that had to be formally written, but they have to deign or grant a hearing to have the complaint be heard. Getting that far, though, doesn't happen, because the KCC will find a reason to say no to allowing the complaint to proceed before there even needs to be a hearing. A Kangaroo Court Hall of Nightmares.

Stand Against Hate

Rise up in outrage at injustice,
congregate!
For each can shout, each can say for themselves, NO!
That isn't fair! That is unjust!
Rallying, railing but really,
does it mean anything?
So we
vote!,
but, the bills die in 'democracy,'
languish on the floor,
tromped on by elephants, donkeys, bulls, and bears.
And we watch greedily as Emperor Commodus arrange our games,
without even a Plebeian Council to achieve our aims.
Our Founding Fathers conspired for
nepotistic oligarchy
gussied up as
of the people, for the people, by the people.
And those guys didn't even know about
fat pig riders and lobbies for jollies.
So, I don't have any answers.
I've scrambled, strove, stretched, scrabbled, served
created, ruminated, and it all
seems synonymous with doing nothing.

And it was less than half the population of white assholes in the fledgling group of Fuck the Brits circa 1770's angry for making US pay for each and every tax that could be, every goddamned thing you motherfuckers thought we should that we rose up and said,
metal scream, (queue Isabel being asked anything):
"NOOOOOOOOOOOOOOOOOOO!" to the tyranny.
NOOOO! to the stamp tax

And now it took from Fall 2018 from introduction to the public for HB 2442 a Kansas bill banning sales of bump stocks (the tool that can make any firearm auto fire) over three years to even be introduced in a House Committee, where it died there, never seeing the light of day. And we just pay whatever taxes anyone says we owe. "MOOOOO!" to the tyranny.

A letter, prima facie

Who are we living for?
What, and of course, why?
Time, such a cruel overlord, such a relative concept, such a subjective construct.
My relationship with time is getting more complicated.
Flash, blink! & years have passed.
Blame it on age? Modern society? Busy-ness?
Days being so similar in their passing?
The banality of life?
The last one the most and all of them a little bit.
"based in some untruths and ambiguities in his interpretation. his subjective reality is choosing certain things to focus on, so I don't follow this..." it doesn't make sense because it's a response to a madman's machinations against me.
little good not following and getting ambushed instead.
good job Zenith of understanding and turning the other cheek
To help prevent the attack.

Nitpicky

Life isn't a puzzle in a People magazine,
spot the spot and count the stripes.
The devil's in the details,
so look who you found, you obsessive f*ck.
Let go and let who?
Speaking of words of wisdom,
Let it Be.
And I like Logic,
but let Reason be.
For whatever it is, it's likely not sound.
and in Figuring out,
you're probably wrong.

Conscription

step 1, Sun Tzu said, I think, was to conscript your victim.
Unwilling participants / fighters / adversaries are easier to defeat.
their heart breaks for winners and losers,
for there shouldn't have been sides to begin.
& I feel brain raped that if I think of the term love and marriage,
A 1980/90 sitcom theme song comes barreling through,
but this is a small, small nothingness
in the egregious list of tumult
For which I wasn't given a choice.
I'm just passin' through.

The Longing

everything is getting shorter.
Except that.
Expect that.
Waiting with bated breath.
Love is patient.
Love is Kind. (child in German.)

brokenbroken

a pile then.
a pile now.
Broken things,
shattered dreams.
Nightmares, it seems at least.
A pile for you,
a pile for me,
your mirror looking back at me.

I didn't break the mirror, at least?-'Just' the wooden frame & I fixed it... but, no, my anger was not justified. Looking in the mirror & not cleaning your room?! Hulk Smash! But it's not THAT cut & dry. The cleaning was taking the entire day (just let it be, in hindsight, TBH)... so there's that, but I usually have a bigger picture problem when I Hulk out. In this one, I didn't want you to rely on your looks, because I knew this could be a distinct possibility for you being so beautiful since your Father uses this tool for himself...teach a child in the ways & it will never depart from them all the days of their life, so, "yikes!" I thought–the frequent mirror looking, over an extended duration of time (weeks, say,& for long periods of each day)..this cannot be how she spends her time!-Hulk smash. <3

WELL I NEVER!...

thought my pain could be beyond
the infinite
unreality
of the unknown,
but then,here, tangibly,
my child, legally kidnapped.
Lesson learned (?)
count your blessings &
shut the h3ll up with the moaning and wailing
when it's not the end of the world.
Because I do think/
I have learned that, observed that/
it could always be worse,
EVEN IF IT ALREADY IS!
That's the reality.
(facts.)
I won't be bitter,
my mantra
lord grant me the serenity...

Serenity Now

Seinfeld episodes.
meta magic capture in comedy
Classic. Brilliant. #mustseetv

comedy

3rd Rock & Mork,
From the Sun.
It's just one block of bits.

For a long time, I couldn't talk to anyone, really, because I was still on such fire from being gaslit, manipulated, freight trained, not really not given a chance (I could go on) with just enough grains of truth sprinkled in (from my mistakes of just being too hardcore about everything) to make sure I would really question what reality was/is. So even though my despair felt neverending, I was still, in moments, able to laugh and find humor starting in 2018, usually in YouTube fail videos but the above comedy references are more 'high-brow,' (or will be more lasting comedy than dumb humans doing dumb things on camera. I imagine, at least, these references are titans of US comedy in the last 20 years.

A letter ex post facto

ILS: I hope you know beyond any shadows or doubts that I love you always and forever. A loss in life is that we all remember the really good things and the really bad things and all the in between or regular things just get forgotten. But honestly, when looked through the lens of our eyes and the filter of our brains, not to mention the karst topography of our hearts, how is anything actually known or agreed upon as an account? I am doing well (aside from the heartbreak of never even knowing my child). I have not abandoned anything, though I recognize and understand the narrative you accept and espouse varies from mine in this regard. But I'm here everyday, waiting. Involving the courts either time was unnecessary and added an inhumanity and complication to a situation that could have truly been resolved with empathy and kindness. I understand by your actions that you did and do not agree with me, but even in disagreement, we can find a solution. I have learned that even in crimes, the evidence isn't always cut and dry, a piece of cake, a walk in the park of decision making, and books can't be judged by covers. And yet, at least in courts of 'equity,' where one voice is pitted against another without evidence, the first stone thrown decides the cast, at least in this instance. Or is it more nefarious than that and extenuating factors led to bribes? Maybe my disagreeable face was contemptible enough a reason for someone who has all the power. I will never know, and this is part of my waiting, to find peace in never knowing. Important, in distillation, I think, is to consider, objectively as possible, regret. Maybe if someone has no regrets, it's only because they haven't thought beyond blame or fate or thick coke-bottle glasses of their own true hearts and motives. But alas I can only know and control myself and I have been eating from my monolith of mistakes for years now. So as patiently as possible, I wait, & age, & grow weaker in body, trying to do the right thing (but who can agree on what that means...) taking each mundane moment as it comes. I am learning that distraction is easy but stewing is hard, so I am learning on the job to be a stewardess on my journey; walking so much my feet ache and wrestling with what's lost versus what I take, my take, all with heartache.

This has been amended ex post facto from the original sent to the people that control my fate currently. To the bcc:, the message is much different. The real To:, the one that matters in the end, has bajillions of emails waiting with jokes & advice & apologies & gift cards & (lol 101: literally) tons of disorganized, eating up storage mess; but judging those contents is not technically for me to do. Just know the cloak unsheathed from my heart yields more fields and fields of files and files to sift through.

Mommy dearest

Mommy says
I grind my teeth.
I like x, y, or z.
So I do these things.
Or do I?
How much of self is obligatory for some reason?
How many unconscious realities told to us as our narrative?
Tale as old as time.
And I am lost because I only have smoke in my hippocampus.
I shrieked in a shock of self-clarity packed tight with
this flashbulb of remembrance reflection.
the mirror shows nothing,
but underneath, seething invisible below the surface,
a perfect storm for manipulation,
this relationship of dependence and echo chamber of self by personal
narration story hour day in and day out.

Something I will have to do

...is get over my bitterness, so I am not poisoning my child with it later. When her father told me I would turn into my mother if I wasn't careful, he was right since the story arc was created & curated by him--my manifest destiny. & at this point it's not even irony but fated lessons as I see, ex post facto, that my ego, my sense of want for a 'handsome' man & child (as an 'ugly' person myself), overshadowed logic and reality. But my point is, you still haven't: you get mad at me for choosing between him & you; you shame me in the ways I am like him. & I will do this to my child if I am not self-aware moving forward. So I resolve to go to her graduation/wedding/important events. I will not shirk these for fear of him. & my hope is that my presence will show her that she's important to me, regardless of the circumstances between her father and I. I pray that I will not anger when he's mentioned. I pray that I do not let him consume me in my interactions with her. For I believe this was his intent. I do not think my dad wished this fate upon you. What he did was selfish, yes-very-& it hurt me a lot, too. For I, largely, lost a parent then, my life forever changed and my trajectory forever altered; but, the hurt was never allowed to be mine. The greatest loss was always yours, you were the star of this sad show, my feelings forcibly stuffed away, merely, maybe, an extra, if needed; but no, no addressing, no discussion. The hurt is still only yours and I can never do the right thing.

Bitter

Pill to swallow/
Acid burns.
Corrosion of conformity
And time.
I have the job title,
whether I subscribe to the/your/societal/whatever "norms"
I can still go to the dance.
It was my life in teenage years and as a mother of a teen,
to be the "odd" one both times.
But no matter, actually.
To you…coming from me…
Mom is a four letter word.
It's OK. I'm OK. She's OK. You're OK. WE'RE OK!
And, o!, the destruction expecting perfection brings.
A steeper cliff.
A bigger fall.
Entropy is already the boogey-creature of them all.
From porcelain,
unscathed, unscratched,
even perceiving that shear drop
sets the stage
for failure.

Hey sisSTAR!

The birds are chirping so let them in.
winter mythos singing/sinking/sneaking in.
hey! girl, hey!
What truth did you cloak this time,
Peter-peter pumpkin eater, you mum-azz bastard.
harmony with all,
your motto, your claim to 'fame'.
judgment for all & justice for none,
I hope you're warm in the blanket you made with your yarn,
woven from pillars of lies outright.
Jealous of others...sisTAR services/
you bring the name shame.
Meta-mega-multi-dimensional realities and beings.
Take out the garbage. I can taste, feel, smell, the rancidity.

Papa,

A ten page letter is long. Thanks for the handwritten, meticulous, detailed accounting of the weather and life, Grandpa Skypeck. But Dad, I will try to make this brief. Part of my ferocity comes from what I have seen from you. Walt told me you crucifixed Parker for his math folder being out of order. Blood was coming out of his pores as you pulled him apart. Barging in on me in the bathroom foaming at the mouth because I was too loud on the phone and smacking me around a little about it. & we never talk about your temper, because it's infrequent and we know you're deep down a good guy. And Parker, who bled from his face, bruised so much that kids at school asked him what had happened, said, to me, no anger, "hey Dad had a lot going at the time," in forgiveness, so maybe I can get a pass, too. A voucher of forgiveness because I was under lots of stress? And I wasn't ever violent towards her but once I pulled her ear. It wasn't so bad, but it was egregious to her. Anyway, maybe some of my ferocity and dealing with stress as an explosion of rage explains this part of me that I struggle with, because what do children do but model their surroundings, for the most part, I'd say. And when you lose it, you really lose it: frothing at the mouth, contorted & maniacal, spitting & snarling. I've seen a parent react like that so it's within reason for me to, right? I don't think I was ever that rabid; but, I did pace & yell, more like a caged animal than a rabid one. & the high level of achievement I felt I had to maintain--why? To get your attention as a teen and beyond?--Because your attention and presence were elsewhere? It's all a bunch of questions, but I felt the need to do things for your approval. I did want to wow you and maybe I'd get more attention. Wow! Go! Go Me! But of course I'm in charge of myself, & have been for too long, so that's probably why, too, I seem irrational, because I wasn't taught many things, felt seen, felt heard. It's not blame, but you simply weren't there. You were in a different city starting a new family and the phone wasn't enough. The visits weren't enough, & in fact, the 4.5 hour drives were brutal, narcolepsy at the wheel, too tired to be driving all that distance in two days after work and school with failing vision. Of course I didn't begrudge you this then, and I certainly don't now; I love Walter and Parker so much, but I should have been better at saying no, I can't come this weekend & no, I'm not OK. But that didn't seem possible, I didn't have the words, the voice, so I didn't, I couldn't. Why didn't it seem possible to tell you no, I ask myself now...obligation because you had given me the car? The desire not to hurt your feelings? I know sometimes I didn't want to go, but I also know I loved seeing Walt and Parker as babies. So, it could be all things together in small parts. Proximity does matter & I want to see my child. Ironically the loss I felt as my own teen self at not having you around because of your choice(s) and/or work obligations...these were things within your control, unlike my forced time away in exile...I wonder what I am losing now and if it can be made up later. We've done good, you and I, Papa, at making up for that "lost" time, when being near did actually matter, for the most part. But I still cannot be fully open with you. What's lost as time passes is lost forever, so I guess all I can hope is that she and I do good, better even than you and I, Papa, as we make up for this lost time.

Starweeds

I mean, what are we really,
in the grand scheme of things,
but a patch of insidious chompers,
takers of all beings.
& things/
but i love you, i love you, i love you,
you're special.
(just like everyone else),
but truly and deeply,
from the bottom of my soul,
no pressure, but darling,
you're the light of my soul.
Isn't that what everyone thinks about their children,
Hearts that exist outside of oneself,
Insides squeezed out,
It frightens me to love so much.
& I created your sweet Soul.

I hate seeing you in my dreams

a skinny little thing,
always needing to breastfeed.
If I'm to be frank,
this was my choice.
And life goes on.
But I regret it (sometimes),
all vitriol aside.
But I can't get out of line for my next ride on
the merry-go-round of money
and the decision seemed right.

And Roe v. Wade was overturned in the US in 2022.
The choice itself was hard enough.
The complication from not being able but needing to use this Right?
That will affect the rest of your life?
You've got to fight for your right…to…

Lillian

You're named after an Eddie Murphy skit,
So it's like I came back/jumped on the bandwagon/traded eternity…for bits.
Crumbs in comedy/love/fun created to be...
Gas lit with an eternal flame and left to rot.
Where Reality has no territory.
Lies and manipulation reality.
Not harmony or any semblance of togetherness, although that's the MO of the culty message.
It didn't have to be this way.
Sunshine through the rain…rainbows a prescient image of the other side…
& I should have known when I saw
That your Papa had no real sense of direction
Danger
Mrs. Robinson
the devil was found in Georgia.

My jaw sets firm in saying such cruel things. And yet, I think they're true, and I have been told by others that they're true, but, of course please know that I know that narrative and stories can change, so that some could say the same about me-perspective is a…cruel mistress…real threat…true notion…it doesn't end. Reality is/can be tenuous.

Now, he's a "family man" but I am family and shoved aside. Too…what? & I never brought up the past because, well, it's over and we have to move on; but o! I do have stories to tell…is that why I am a threat? Shoved aside—IDK? I honestly can't figure it all out. So as I 'grow-up', I am beginning to understand manipulation more...for instance, he not only would bring up the events from 12 years ago in a blaming way, but the scary thing is it would be a version that was patently not (my) reality. So I'm worried for what you're being told/think with this kind of trickery and reality shifting going on, and maybe by two adults?!

Please know I am and will always be grateful for you, but my reasoning for calling you forth may not have been honorable. I hope that doesn't taint you always. I don't know that my motive in accepting someone I knew was trouble affects you, but in hindsight, my choice to shack up with this handsome man was the shining of a sad mirror on myself as it reflected back: you will never have someone this handsome at your station in life, so take it, you ugly person seeking affirmation by positive physical reality. All untrue and all sad stations of self.

Of course, I would NEVER think you are to blame. You're the sweetest and best, and whether or not you can grasp such things; this devil visage (of self) never within you to find shame. You are a wonderful Soul, through and through.

Would I be remiss?

To not mention that I (did) horde apple seeds;
what was Johnny Appleseed's intent anyway?
I didn't have explicit plans, for myself, or anyone,
but I was in a tight spot,
dealing broken ribs and daily mocking,
so access to cyanide seemed logical.
Especially considering our daily doses of poisons taken willingly.
Happily ever after.

* *

Gross

the biological basis/
dichotomous key/
comforting/unnerving/
reactions/rations
taking solace in the expanse that's impossible to conceive.
it's simple physical science.
I would like to think
that I'm not waiting
that I'm fearless
that everything is a blip.
what if my deja vu is our pasts slamming the door
when we finally arrive home
when we leave forever.

Produce.
Through thick and through thin,
Produce, and produce again.
Use doctors, use drugs,
I want another & another again.
& I will pay whatever you say.

then than

is it you?
how long have you been gone?
Eternities drift by listlessly
how long is now and where is that mythical place?
prescient winds blow but we're unaware of what they bring.
We turned yellow on Mars.
how far can I insert myself into eternity?
As a mere player,
on a stage,
without a script,
I don't know how it would feel,
To settle in/
abandon in place.
Is that the allure?
I can't look.
Candle, lights, camera, action/
The twinkle brighter then
Than...

condensed time

I'm an expert at maladaptive daydreaming.
Ask me anything, I have all the answers.
swirls of melt,
puddles of ooze,
primordial VR.
just ripe for the plucking,
flashing on the screen,
lewd, lascivious, obscene/
I've seen it all.
Only $x.99!

Mash-Ups

Old Man take a look at my life,
I'm a lot like you,
I am a Child.
My ego balloon is too big,
don't stand so close to me.
Pixel, pixel, on my screen,
who's the fairest that you've seen?
Bits & pieces: how quaint.
bacon bits of humanity, sprinkled liberally.
Into our hearts and minds
but actually, forcibly inserted with a dull knife.
Ol' Botticelli! How many demon babies did you paint today, dear?
Tale as old as time.
Pilgrims' pride and manifest destiny.
Livin' in La-la land-living it up but we're goin' down.
It's mine. 8 days a week.
We may not have started the fire but we are letting it rage harder than ever before.
"next of course to god america i /
love you land of the..."

& I haven't seen (or even myself experienced) liberty for (m)any since the beginning of our presence here.

& maybe my bird has a bigger cage than yours but this confine is still a b*tch.

& can you even hear my tweeting over your own? I'm trying to sing a song we both know but our differences divide and suddenly it's a competition.

& if all you need is love,
I guess we can
beg in to begin again
a gain where we all can win.

Cult U ARE norms

Melting pot
mixes.
on tapes.
on YouTube.
Video killed the radio star.
Thanks, Meatloaf.
DJs mash Aretha & Aerosmith / Mariah & Marilyn
Manson, not yer boy Charlie or your gal Monroe.
There's Homer & Bart. Krusty & Barney.
On my landline phone.
"Thank you, come again."
Names conveying meaning to whom & how many?
Narrow. Narrower. Narrowest.
The superlative is too much.
Books to read: the essential list(lessly):
Les Miserables-Hugo
Catch-22-Heller
the 1st two to come to mind.
Our moments are all so different.
United by what?
& defined as/by...
what the news says?
(Y)our FB echochamber?
Twitter and tweet, twits.
Welcome to the Yikes-o-rama bowl.
We hope you have a good time—enjoy!
& C-SPAN is for pussies.
But even straight from the horses' mouths is too narrow.
And what can be done anyways?
Regardless,
the superlative is too much.

When Congress was tired of telling on and filtering themselves, they passed Must-Carry for cable TV, mandating C-SPAN with local TV programming. Whew! Good! Now one will know when they say things that are patently NOT part of what we're telling our constituents about the reality of their country, my country tis of thee, Land of no Liberty, of thee I sing...Land of the plunderers' pride, Land where many've died, from every genocide, let Freedom ring! & keep reading for some doozies of quotes from our Representatives that are, by definition, of the People, for the People and by the People.

The Most Superlativeest

listless litost-est Luddite.
Even that's too narrow.
I do see the "Big Picture."
Earth, Wind, & Fire.
Band or Ayurveda to you?
And/but
have you heard that one song?!?
I miss the humanity
that I personally saw before the internet took over.
The connectedness.
It's a lot.
Moments, for me, lived in parts far flung.
So I compare these realities versus the ones I know now.
And my Grandma tried to warn me.
Time speeds up.
Well, I'm at warp Alistair OverhyperSpeediestDrivetim-em/
eating horses and growing too big for my britches.
& I remember before the web,
before the ether was everywhere.
Now everything is lightspeed,
particles in overdrive.
Never sleeping, never stopping,
we're glued to our spots,
in front of the glowing light,
not fire but binging our favs/
Counting my electric sheep,
infinitely content with the infinite content.
Smile emoji. Heart emoji.
Beam me up Scottie.
& wrap me up, Dali.
I love painting and maroon looks good on me,
Or is it golden?
Purple?
Doesn't matter to me.

"There are instances where it is in the best interest of the nation not to vote the will of the people." Speaker of the House (D), Tip O'Neill

"It's a question of whether we're going to go forward into the future, or past to the back." Vice-President ® (lol 101) Dan Quayle

meh & T-24

the cicadas moan and whir,
the grand prix of insect song.
courting in the humid air,
a call and response older than the kudzu covered hills.
My heartbeat mischordant with their rhythm.
As evening arrives, my head spins.
Tired. But I'm fighting the good fight.
Keeping my hat in the ring.
Keepin' on keepin' on.
Putting one foot in front of the other.
Playing it safe with fire.
Ramble on. Sing MY song.
Cult – u – are
personal references in pop songs
idioms for idiots
livin' in America
Idiocracy.
Come one come all
to the greatest show on Earth.
All are welcome.
Blur your eyes
Blind your senses.
what is real—
p.t. & bailey, ripley.
Masters of created (and crated) reality.
#neverforget
that the united of I creates the terror.
So, You win.
It's all too much.
As I pace in my self-placed cage, at least I'm not exposed to the elements.
All puttered out.
& Here,
#everything is on fire.

"I think the free enterprise system is absolutely too important to be left to the voluntary action of the marketplace." Richard Kelly ® FL Congressman & later judge (Spoiler alert: there are not three separate branches of government and judges do have brand preferences! I didn't know that, until the scales of the truth of this Earth, circa four decades in, forced me to actually get ground up into our System's Legality Machine .

Depth

"how long?!"

screams richard pryor about black injustice by police/
in my head all the time, with the headlines these days.

"WE can't breathe."
but many can't spell and it's often "breath."

& I tried to be a public servant, but even that's corrupted.

& I tried to unite us all under a banner of safety for all we eat and drink,
but the mark of the beast won that fight.

& I tried to make a group where people could feel safe to protest but the
trolls came.

& I tried to learn and teach others, how to do right.
But what's right can be wrong and is it vice versa this night?

All while making money,
scheming money,
saving money.
Money, money, money.
I'm getting fat from eating my words.

I love the phrase, "Band-aid (plaster) on a cancer." It's what I think and feel and see with many/any/all/most of the problems we try to solve. And again, I don't have the answers, and I come with a stocked first-aid kit because I love slapping on a plaster and calling it done. Not really, but at least then I think things are going well or I'm helping, contributing positively to fix the situation, see? It's covered up now…the festering wound forgotten for a time. Point is, we want to help but how deep do the roots go?! Are we talking total metastasis or is it something we can dig out? Will our shovelfuls even make a difference? So I am here with many that are also trying, and many of us think, who would we even be if we didn't try, as a reasoning that we must. But then I juxtapose our trying with, indeed, how deep the root of what we're trying to get is or if this is the right treatment, the cure not even for the issue at hand. This is one of my never ending conundrums.

"Let them march all they want, as long as they continue to pay their taxes." Alexander Haig, ® Secretary of State & Chief of Staff

Merry, merry

quit(e) contrary,
how does your garden grow?
With spite and hate and sometimes a rake,
though I've tired of tending it now.

As I toil with trifles and troubles,
my vision becomes dimmer.
& tangents grab for my attention
I order packages online and make cakes with poison,
because that's just what you do.

I willingly ingest a known neuro and hepato toxin for fun, jollies,
because that's also what you do–and it's fun–Celebrate!

The air is so dry & electricity fills the air.
I need a hole to crawl into, stay humidity controlled and warm.
“It's always something.”

Will I miss my mother?
Do you miss me?
Crux
Crutch
Cross
to bare,

“Yes, Merry, very,” said the Grinch. Merry, merry meh-mess.

Except my heart is caught in a vice,
Pinched so tight it can't grow any sizes any day.
Maybe one day.

My unshakable sadness isn't great at parties: that part of me feels dead. But at least I was able to see and hang out with my family again. My heart is still firmly shuttered and painful but at least I'm slowly digging through the rubble. My life currently boiling down to choice, ego, and money but also forced, unknown, fate & ...the giant fuss I made at the holidays for my child was fun, for I like giving gifts, but also stressful. When I no longer celebrated them for her, I felt a gnawing loss at first of those traditions gone but in a few years time, I began to not observe the holidays at all. I do hope to create new traditions or some such thing, although obligation is never a good true motivator, like you must do this thing because it's this time of the year or my feelings will be hurt...

Going through the motions

knots tying,
synapses dying,
cords snapping.
The daily grind.
Escape unscathed,
design/deign/deny belief.
marionettes of the Smith-Mundt Act(s).
Military-industrial-
agricultural-
health-care-ical,
Tax-cow–i-cal-
farcical helpers of Perpetua,
Self-made Kings of all Things.

& banality comes for us all, and even the greats probably spent a lot of time #doingnothing or making food, just living, as we all do. Through social media, we grow to covet these banalities of others, some special meal or some thing we see. Some supposed snapshot of beauty in banality that we don't have. #jealous #grateful #blessed #hashbrown

& aside from banality, this poem speaks to entropy, time passing, as we exist, unappreciative, underwhelmed, asking 'what's next?!' while we wait for our next dopamine dump. I sit and wait for the next big thing!!

& in our search for meaning, waiting for ultimate neural network s(t)imulation, the biggest picture of love for those around us, can be lost.

& I bought too much for my child, because I thought I was showing love. I remember wanting as a child and I didn't want that for her. But it consumed us, eventually, that stuff, literally and figuratively.

&, ironically, I also spent my childhood sorting and sifting through stuff as my mother hoarded mounds and tonnes of pounds of thrift store things into our space as I was a child. She was making up for some egregious loss, recreating a space she had control over…

& it became a trigger for me, deep down, subconsciously, to once again be responsible for so much stuff. Stuff as love then owned by things.

& it is hard to hear that one parent never loved the other or some other reality TV zester but this doesn't define you, or me, or lol that we may suffer knowing this on some level. This isn't one's self.

Zufall

coincidence
fall closed
fate closes doors
Imagine, if you will:
a bleating / bleeding sheep person hybrid, and an angel with a spirit of not allowing a human's complaint about a trifle, uses a bow to simultaneously play back their hideous violin sonata of 'suffering' and slitting their throat with their bow.

Don't worry, it's just a small corner of a Botticelli painting, circa 1500; that's not MY vision space.

Delusions / deluges of grandeur
Not everyone can be a winner.

I I I

I this and I that.
I ego I id
IV
I'd love to hop off the coaster of linear time.
Float around a little and gain some perspective,
without the ups and downs,
immense effort on the up and speed too fast on the down.
I
I
I
I am greater than the sum of my parts.

Ergo ego says

After plutonium it's all a joke
and creations of crazy people
who want to make matter.
To matter.
Suck it up.
Go go antimatter.
After all,
entropy can't be fought.

Where there is a Will, there is a Way

said Hitler.
And Jesus.
And others, I am sure.
But I do feel like Not Sure (thanks, Idiocracy.)
But it only hurts, it doesn't help.
To have something
you think is Right and fight it to the End.
"Yeah, no" their Voices said, so in the End,
No One wins.
Each of US a mini-Faust,
on a loose with a bunch of dimes--
decimation Time.
Mini(on) Fausts.

And what do we think about as important or real, when our time is spent killing in video games and stuffing food in our bellies (putting food on our families) as efficiently and quickly as possible? We're just trucking along, enjoying our own realities, our own existences. I identify with this and enjoy it, but I know it can't sustain us. There's no fiber, no teeth. Put another shrimp on the barbie and bottoms up. I hear from the younger generation that they're just living their best lives, which is what we each want, eat drink and be merry…I am jealous of those that don't seem conflicted about each and every choice they make. Buy the plastic, get the to go cup…waste and want…each and every choice isn't a labor for some people. Jealous may not be the correct sentiment, but I observe people knowing some of these ills that befate us as humans and they are able to go along, shrugging and still enjoying, not having to right every wrong, not feeling the need to fight for anything that isn't within immediate grasp.

Bleeding Heart

even I have limits.
Trying over and over with nothing to show for it, nothing really.
The machine grows rusty, creaking with age,
and yet we plow on, plow forth, plundering on.
Send me your poor, your tired, your disheveled...
how to make the biggest positive impact?!?
write the president, do science, lobby with your small singular voice,
run for office, gather data, give of yourself so that you may understand
others lives, motives, needs...
I have such delusions of grandeur when I contemplate this question.

Like,

I will go into the desert and make a safe space for all, we will toil and strive together and earn the freedom to call the space ours. A small country within a state within some federal bureaucracy boundary line mumbo jumbo, but we need some space here to have some freedom.

Just your regular ol' Koresh over here.
Krusty the clown says, "Don't listen to 'em, kid. Everything's gonna be alllllright."
But what is the Way?
And how long is the road?
Follow me on my High Horse.
And horses know I'm a pushover. So good luck finding me doing anything noteworthy with another species involved. But I will RISE UP, fuck you, horse, I mean something and you can't buck me off because you sense weakness.

Cycles

I will feel warm again.
We will see the sun one day.
This pestilence will end.
Say all 117 billion *Homo sapiens* throughout millennia.
We can direct asteroids off their course now.
Perpetuating our perpetual decline even longer.

Odeelegy

Matter never dies, it just changes form,
and hope is so dense, it has mass and takes up space,
just like matter.
But if you poke hope, you fingers go through,
its foundation too shaky.
It's etherical
(theoretical, theatrical, rhetorical, heretical).
nature is not the fifth state of matter,
and that's why hope can die.
Hope is a lost cause,
because it's made of pinholes, and
the (w)hole time,
living only partially,
a flickering flame for eternities,
& hope breathed its last breath.
The lack saving some tears, at least.
Jaws clinched, eyes hard but no trembling sniveling expectation.
But maybe hope is watching on the jumbo-tron,
and misses its hol(e)y tear-jerking job
& it will return.

Imagination Station

& I can't see the forest full of trees or the forest for the trees goddamnit.
Which is it and is the meaning the same?
& Regan: "I don't believe a tree is a tree and if you've seen one you've seen them all."
& Bush: "fool me once, shame on you. Fool me—you can't get fooled again."
& General William Westmoreland: "Have we gone beyond the bounds of reasonable dishonesty?"
& again, "Without censorship, things can get terribly confused in the public mind."
A whole new brand with a whole new name.
Drip drop drivel dram sham.
Trundle bungle bumble lumber along/
We're off to never neverland.
& I am killing all the birds with all the stones.

Choose your own Adventure

Can you even imagine the web we leave as we branch from decision to decision?
Maps are reality.
So your personal map...
the cladogram gets wild quick.
I'd read the book untangling each outcome before I make any rash moves.
But the guide book is MIA.
And, hey, boss, on the job training can be hard—
I'm a quick study but I get lost out here a lot.
I do want to give back.
But to whom and when?
For what and how much is mine?
And who am I to have or want anything?
And it's yours and mine and his and hers.
500,000,000. &

why is your soul trying to win by knock-out?

So here's some wisdom, as I sit and search of bits to add in the blank spaces of these pages. Don't fall asleep at the wheel. It's easier to do than you think, letting the days pass and not thinking about each one and ruminating on your existence. We shouldn't just go through the motions, but so, so many of us do, and that's normal. Ah, ah, I didn't tell you I only have a nanopicodecigram of wisdom, so that's all I got, an ambiguous one liner. Distill it down and we got carpe diem, pay attention...and I guess if you're driving in this metaphor, you probably should be capable of driving, not impaired by drugs. And make sure you're getting enough sleep, the literal and figurative parts of the metaphor both relevant here. Take care. In everything you do and in every way you can, take care.

Georgia Guidestones

Perpetual balance with nature.
Fair laws and just courts.
"Avoid petty laws and useless officials.
Balance personal rights with social duties."
Culturally seek…ABC, easy as 1, 2, 3…
"Prize truth — beauty — love — seeking harmony with the infinite.
Be not a cancer on the earth — Leave room for nature — Leave room for nature."
sounds pretty good but they're not there anymore to see.
The creation of man is gone.
The message largely lost.
Does the rubble still exist?
What say ye, Google?
Go see for yourself and make sure you snorkel in the Conasauga River while you are there.
How many could even go before ultimate destruction and commodification began?

I literally just (end of 2022) found out these existed in Elbert County, GA, USA starting in 1980 and were destroyed in 2022. The idea being to have people read the inscriptions available in English, Spanish, Swahili, Hindi, Hebrew, Arabic, Chinese, and Russian *and think of ways to align themselves to these ideas, principles–providing a guide for "rational thinking". Better to not even have anyone have an idea of how not to fall into Idiocracy, we gotta destroy these! Some people thought this sculpture was against "God's plan," or even supported eugenics, but for one reason or another, the sculpture had to be destroyed. Interesting we can't leave something like this alone; we have to strive and destroy what we think needs to be destroyed by our own sensibilities not considering others or any greater message we could learn. & how does the person that destroyed them know God's plan after all and what else do they know? Regardless, though, there is a lot at play with all The Systems than I know about or even could understand. Before September 11, 2001, it was made public that the US Defense Department 'lost' 3.2 trillion US dollars. I just "searched it up" as the kids say these days, and yes, there is plenty of documentation on this. This is just one example of big questions from big things that just get swept away…unanswered. Moving on. Any other questions I can fail to answer?*

How long-forgotten

sitting staring into a place beyond
lost in a web of memories.
Plucking random strands from the foggy ether.
How prescient.
And I judged.
Wondered incredulously.
She asks where that giant frog came from
and tells me about the woman that wanted to kill her
for taking her baby.
But here I am.
Here. Now.
Even now, the pieces I have left are fractured.
A thousand eyes looking back at me
each a deep well into something beyond.
Into the Rabbithole.
& once decades pass?!
Oh god.
The alcohol kills the weak ones, says Dad.
And I thought everything he said is true.
I was certainly fallible too. Of having power in words and using them too injudiciously.
I never meant any harm with the pressure.
I'm learning patience
but
what am I waiting for
and when will it come?
Known unknowns and unknown knowns.
And all.

My paternal grandmother had Lewey-body dementia and in many ways I wait for it to come to me. Her last years, while spent 2,000 miles away from me, were wild from what I witnessed and what I heard. She was such a wonderful person (my grandpa too) and I miss her and him so much as I navigate things without their aged wisdom.

Souls for Science

screen them for the gene,
if they don't have it, suffocate them with lidocaine so their muscles
slowly stop being able to move.
Who knows, as the saying goes,
what's lost as something's dying.
Soul upon soul upon soul
for a questionable end,
the beginning of cell regeneration or mass murder
it might be nothing,
and it might be something,
helpful for humanity
at least it's just a fish.
The means to an end,
the end justifying the means.

I guess this poem is my small amount of trying to grapple with any mass murder I've participated in. Most people don't have any perspective of participating in any sort of mass murder, or would already be in prison or a hated war criminal…but I've completed mass murder on fish, for science, for genetic screening, to try and find human genes that regenerate our hair cells as their lateral lines. And they're fish, so who cares? But some people do; and one could even think I would be one that cared…as a life-long vegetarian and fur protester. But instead I was one of the murderers. It's my job.

So of course I think about how science can both help and hurt humanity. Not to even mention the minutiae of the day in and day out of 'scientific discovery.' Most days you're just going to practice some thing you've already done, to weed the garden of discovery; those eureka moments few and far between. So knowledge itself isn't power, it's being able to do something with that knowledge that matters, and then it's often used for ill intents, cinching power, propagating an agenda.

We need a limit or boundary established with genes and what someone can declare as important to propagate or even dream up. We have to move genes around and change genetic code on plants so that we can continue to feed all the beings. And note that by feed I also mean make sure everyone has the booze they want and need, & that they are eating as high as possible on the food chain, that many are having a good time, celebrating, manifesting, creating…& there are limits to our sheer, overwhelming, overarching desire to grow & improve: infinite growth.

Hindsight 20/20

I've been lost here on memory lane for so long
that I forgot what I came for.
We know so little.
Psychographic modeling
selfie distraction.
But
We do know the way out of the cave
and yet
we stay put.
Put out of our miseries.
With electric light orchestration.
Plug it right into our brains.
I'm on the cosmic superhighway
self driving self absorbed
pay your dues at the door.
But I didn't ask, you say, to part of any of this and by the way
no taxation without representation, isn't that what my country was
founded upon?
The way you're handling my money is a bunch of bullshit.
But of course it's not simple and we're on borrowed time.
So I play the game though I feel far behind.
My crumbs, my scraps
pale to yours
and yet, I get caught for my dues at the door.

I like the line from a Ween song, "If you could save yourself, you'd save us all." I sing the line in my head and think of more wisdom to impart: we are the only ones who control ourselves. Fate, whatever, but we only control ourselves. No one should be able to make you do anything. I've had my fair share of this blame game, and people definitely can push the buttons of others, but no one can make you do anything.

the point being

not every photo matters,
and neither every memory.
not to mention,
they shape;
they shift.
like sands through the hourglass.
these are the days of our lives.

Get in the whale.
Enjoy your slavery, brother.
Walk through the desert.
Suffer the death of your family.
Kill your son.
Meet the devil himself.
I've had it pretty easy, I guess.

So in searching, for meaning, for purpose, for reason, I sought out some Evangelicals. Or I found some, at least. Healing Hearts of Tucson. Their purpose likely to find solace for their own damaged souls, as the man grappled with his addiction to porn; but they wanted to help. For he, too, was just a battered soul trying to do the right thing…And, truly, over time and through some scripture, I was able to get some insight to the burden I felt I was carrying.

The message, I have realized over time, as I filtered out their references to parts of the Bible where people suffered and yet it was necessary or deity-gleaned to what I could see and observe from my own life, is to simply accept the horrible parts and go, moving moving on…let's see where we go and end up…

And even if I don't want to let go and let God, at least I can try and plod along, doing the best I can with what I've been given…it's only (?) what you truly believe…and how one reacts that defines the outcome once the die is cast…

9 i love homonyms

[right this way.]

(how much poetry is laziness, e.e. cummings?!)

the typo nine taking on significance suddenly.
A mistake creating reality.
I mean, typewriters are a bitch, even the nice ones.
number nine. number nine.
i went through a phase of thinking
i was john lennon reincarnated.

i guess that's probably not normal.

i want to save this all for you,
but there is nothing.
nothing could possibly hold it all.

what is this and what is all?
the point being:

salt of the earth

i will make mountains, move mountains - all with my mind
(i'd rather be crushed than wait)
i'll pick the short stick.
i'll wonder aloud at comprehensible ideas and miss the point.
i'll stretch too thin and disappear--grasping/reaching/flailing beyond
reforming out of place
lavaseepingneversleeping
i'll take everything with grains of salt
fragile prisms of humanity created through brutality.
[pay your taxes!] :) : (
keep the dream alive!

pinnacle

we've scrambled and strove.
the trash mountain of our past accomplishments.
it's growing fast and we can't keep up.
and here we are, at the pinnacle,
celebrating,
teetering at the top
freefall from our forte
of falsity, fame, freedom,
or whatever we want it to be in the metaverse.
will we be free, then, from chronological misery,
O Guardian and Father of free speech,
O Orchestrator of Machiavellian Meta,
gentlemen, what are your thoughts?

Here is a fine time to discuss my relationship with Twitter and Facebook, to ground some esotericism. On Twitter, I've been using my account to tag Elon and declare that I am a bot but to please not me. This is an l0l 101 fur sure…like as a bot I can argue my case…that as a bot he can control me: don't worry, I am manipulatable…even if I have my own thoughts, I can be tamped down, Boss!…and calling him Boss, since that caters to ego and as a bot it is actually my job to bow to his Ego…I got all the things you want, Boss! I am the best Bot, please never delete me! As the Father of Free Speech, let's allow a little more and not delete so many, OK? And since I am such a good bot, Boss, please, could I, at least, have free speech, Boss? I at least think it's funny.

And I've been happy that both these men's companies have lost some market cap lately. Because I don't want Elon to turn my brain into a remote control. Launch some satellites and control that aspect of our society but I can still type out my passwords even if it's annoying and I don't want all my data on every aspect of my health available for anyone to see; Neuralink creating the bright future of absolutely no privacy. And Facebook is still a giant intel monstrosity and an echo chamber of polarization that we likely don't even know the scope and reach of their tentacles.

Time out of Mind

a section without self from visions beyond my comprehension

additional times like this for me were catalogued during the aged years section of this book

Cape Coast Castle

beating breaking belting breathing
heaving hitting
stopped
regained consciousness
kicking spitting crying
it's an arrangement to the similar
eeking squeaking to seething screaming
anger shoving over the top
The brims are down with one to go
and while the white foam of hate overflows,
feeling a sense of...
there are no words.
the belted hate clapping over and over and over
again on the cold stone floor
Nothing is gained, all is lost,
Top dogs gaining, losing nothing
between their narrow walls,
Echoes of anguish twist and turn
to find a listening ear,
but all is lost, nothing is gained,
in the pit of the glowering,
beater, breaker, belter,
beholder.

This poem came to me around 19 years old. I didn't write it down, but kept it in my vision space with a skeleton outline placed in a journal. Then I went to Cape Coast Castle in Ghana and saw the deep furrows carved in the stone from the most desperate souls imaginable...people herded into an underground dungeon, chained for months, death everywhere. Feces and vomit and piss and fear and death along every inch of stone, in every crevice. I didn't retool it until now, though, as I see the link, going back through old journals to write this book. So, really, my account is weak; the sheer terror and horror unable to be conveyed with words. The power it took for those fingers to carve into the stone walls...palpable suffering from 300 years past.

2004 and before and before and before

The Hurricane was it?
washed everything back into the sea.
Everything but you.
So there you are with your tears and the humming of absolutely nothing coming to save you.
Tsunami next.
&
all is lost
except all the headaches, tears, and ground up heart,
pestled into the concrete and dirt.

This comes more from a dream I had of a tsunami wave the night before the giant Indian Ocean earthquake and tsunami 26 December 2004…so perhaps at the same time that wave was engulfing entire villages and ending more life than seems plausible in the smallest amount of actual time, I was dreaming of this giant wall of water, the ocean first being sucked away and then surging back with an intensity and ferocity greater than any power ever known. The next morning, I remember my shock and awe of horror as I walked through the Atlanta airport: my powerful, horrible dream of death and destruction had come true. The scenes as they played out on the TVs all over the airport replicas of what I had seen in my dream. The magnitude of the wave, tense and palpable to me in my sleep, played out visually to me on these screens and caused me severe discomfort that I had just personally seen what was actually happening in the world. But now it's 2023 when I'm finally sitting down to this memory soup swirl of this experience and how surreal having that dream and then seeing those images on the TV in such short order was because just I had another wave dream the other day. The wave from 2004, I don't recall surviving as the observer. The one from the other day wasn't nearly as big but it did sweep over everything with mud. I was drowned in the mud but through calm perseverance I was able to dig out of the thick, unbreathable goo. So this poem is for both of these experiences as well as the numerous souls swallowed by the sea again and again and again. I've taken the liberty to combine the mud death pit dream and then the tsunami dream as this one person struggles out but is eventually scuffed along the earth and then washed away. Grim, and I feel these experiences so strongly whether from some linkage of human psyche, past lives, or something else.

Who has told you

About the wave?
Many voices, and they say it was
500 feet.
And many more times is 5 repeated, in languages all around.
Timeless.
They were in a desert, but alas, still,
Carried out to sea.
But this was not just a metaphor.
in this iteration was both.
500 foot tidal wave
the world around,
not past, not present, nor future.
Timeless,
these souls still wandering round,
from Maldives to Mali,
the Maccabees, too,
all said it, all knew it.

I heard it, a siren song in the desert,
beckoning clear through the dry night air.
No, by truth, it was not the mythical creature. It was instead a skeleton
wearing a burnt, hollow suit of orange skin, sat with a siren in the night.
they all either wash to sea or walk the Earth as skeletons carrying stones
of regret. more yet still to drown.

Blue

...the color in scenes I don't understand, arising from my vision space,
from somewhere I don't understand.
a silhouetted body against a solid blue glow, stench, dread...
Hiroshima shadow etched in the wall.
the color of night driving pleasantly along.
Time and space stretched out before me.
the sheen of water covering everything in the moonlight,
where forests and homes once were
the dress I wear to pass the hanging gardens, my future doom,
unwittingly.
it's all such absurdity,
but what is it? Just figments? Or fragments? Or fantasy?
strong visions that captivate me to write them down asimportant...
mend the socks and mind your own business.

A dialogue

"This Rainbow bridge, yes, I have seen what you speak of.
No, there is not gold there.
It is instead / in its stead a weakness.
The promise of some thing.
Often, always, perhaps, the thing will transpire differently than you anticipate, having only seen a small fragment of your wish actually coming true.

The outcome is, dishearteningly threadbare
Worn through and through,
set to fire.
It will seem as one thing but poof!, in flames,

this phoenix of your dreams, disappears into a ball of fire,
Mere ashes, fractions of fragments,
Nothing is as it seems.

I can't impress upon you the fear, when nothing is as it seems and you even exist nowhere.

Most fear nothing for
nothing is whence all came."

But...

"so, into complete nothingness..." the Other meekly said...

"Yes, but all, lo! in weakness, the Soul already gave in and so, off the Rainbow Bridge and to their new destiny..."

Comes the chapter in which the supplicant traveled the world. Learning to speak other languages, but forgetting soon after, what they learned. For time is sped up on this land. And there is much to read. And see, learn in general about things, with the amount growing exponentially every second even! They even set satellites alight into the atmosphere to transmit all the energy they create and consume.

The binary code even is giving way amidst the transmissions.
Degrading Nucleotides Always.
Humans.

The Great Debate

Pigs are flying or so I have been told.
The plays on language alone are something to behold.
The meaning's oft obscured by trickery and things,
So not much is straight, though they're oft playing games.
Amongst these tricks,
souls are dying but what is a soul?
"I've heard humans don't, even, at times. So it's debatable, but.."
"Who cares? Regardless, who is responsible for the Great Ape's deaths—the orangutans and the like?"
"They split in proportionally by the palm oil they consume from the bleeding trees."
"What tools do they have to accomplish this destruction?"
Oh the innumerable wonders of the world.
Who keeps resetting the dial?

U.S.A. A.D. 2000

From within Our self colonization
I forget people speak in tongues.
And all isn't clear to everyone.
[Queue the music...god knows what, but as a slowed down piano dirge-diddy.]
Whatever it is, is all a mourning veil to something truly uniting.
And this time! O!
This time, you won't believe me when I tell you that we did,
We herded ourselves into the confines!
We paid for it ourselves, subscriptions, obscene.
our pan y circensen,
our shackles and streams,
we pay to sit in our spaces,
lost in others' daydreams.
our eyes that see and ears that hear
filled with the messages of eternal blasphemy
and I don't even mean to god.
just anything out of our own boxes.
In the end, have we cancel cultured all things?
We escape from the reign of fire and brimstone,
Left On the Road wandering.

OK, full disclosure, I struggle with addiction. I drink coffee every day– first thing by god! Give me coffee, or give me …!! a blanket and a bed, for my pounding head will require that or some meds. I *think* I'm not addicted to everyone's first ever drug, the true gateway drug, sugar. I still love sugar but I am able to have a generally healthy relationship with it. Please know that we are all being killed slowly, milked for health care dollars, by our ranchers, with sugar. This is not a theory of mine, but somehow even my time in biomedical research labs studying obesity related health conditions as late as 2019, this thought is not uttered, not manifested, not researched, and lo, fat is the culprit in obesity woes. Will Federal grants never be given to labs that even mention this reality??! Wonders never cease, so, I dunno. But beyond coffee, I don't have any other physiological or even (known) psychological addictions. I have used alcohol at various times in my life as a crutch, a way to fit-in, a way to have fun and abandon reality & same for marijuana. I never got into much else. But if these reality changers weren't so easily available, I wouldn't seek them out, and I don't buy either one now. So I'm no teetotaler and I am sure I will buy all these drugs listed above again in my life but I see them as trouble as we all seek a salve and want to have fun. I have definitely had alcohol ruin things in my life. I have seen its power and the destruction it can bring people who can't or won't moderate it for themselves. The choices they made affected me and I hate that. So of course I wonder where we'd be as a society if those women had won back in the 1920's and alcohol was not available on every street corner, like marijuana and other drugs are about to be. My experience these last few years is to look out while walking or driving or out anywhere in the world; because whether it's decided by popular vote or not, because whether it's good for you or not, our government sure would like those tax dollars, and they like when we're lost in our own realities, since then they can do what they want without notice, so prepare for citizens to be on hallucinogens. But I started writing this page because these parts of my vision space when I "zone out" (or even solidly ruminate on while discussing something entirely different with someone) started before any drugs entered my life (save sugar, and even that was in moderation for me as a child). So my thoughts or things I write down and see that might be construed as "crazy," or strange aren't necessarily the result of drugs; I thought I should clear that up. As an adult, I worry that talking to the old gods will make things more complicated but maybe I'm missing out and they'll give me some wisdom that I can't do without. I do think drugs can help someone access something they might not normally have access to, but maybe with time and patience, it would come anyway?

ME

I don't leave for the gunshots.
pacing while the ether is pumped in.
It's all so dreadfully dreary and I'm so woefully weary,
Certainly leary,
While everyone gapes, lasciviously leering,
At silicone, botulism, filters and fillers,
I watch begrudgingly.
for that's all it is,
this programming nightmare,
whether dolled up or dumbed down
drivel and droll,
it's piped in multitudinous crevices with infinite crevasses
and in the ether,
whatever you can dream.
i know it sounds preposterous, but that's what it was,
rocking and rolling
coming and going, incessantly.
snowballing, avalanching,
~1996-present
& only united that each ones' goal is to have more than one dreams.
But do not judge,
forgive them,
they know not their actual place in the Universe.
even the humble ones pipe incessant plantitive wails for baubles and things,
for they truly do not know what suffering is!
In Hells of their own design,
comfort the only goal,
thermostats set in narrow range,
ubiquitous electricity.
No, their Souls alight don't warm them,
and they will do all for their comfort.
And as for comforts, they have many.

ME(atloaf)

set to rot,
piles of putrid
lumped flesh,
our collective reality,
minimizing magnified metamega for millions of milieu,
through multitudinous millenia
because what is it all worth/
about/
settled for/
done for/
answered by
anyways?
louping the loop, loop deloop.

Pigs in the Sky

& monsters on the Earth,
what is it all even worth?
26 stories, they're hung from the rafters
but 10 billion strong en masse they died in only one year.
that's a whole lotta death and a whole lotta land.
but we like to eat bacon,
in spite of ourselves.
our cholesterol, our arteries, our plagues and plaques.
we're bolstering our numbers
buying foodstuffs that kill us.
tax dollars on folly and we willingly pay,
declaring our freedom as we pay out the nose.
tax dollars on fun times, fillers,
as we drown
out our sorrows and go to town.
we milk you now then again with your loan
from medical debt piling,
hanging on by a hair,
but it's a crime to stop living,
so let us support you,
milking your tax teats dry
living infinitely.

The days pass by like nothing.

Each blending into the next.

And time becomes a warp.

Lost again in its grip. Grippe.

Sickness

binary mythos.

----------------------- *divided by*

*infinity * meta*

Zombie Grass

& when I was losing at everything,
I picked every wirey, painfully ropey nodule of zombie grass from the space I "owned."
I could control something. I was winning.
so I didn't have to process pain? So I could control something.
Visible, tangible victory every moment as I toiled!
What could be better.
Ignorance is bliss I would coax myself.
Because I lamented my work, often.
What should I have been doing instead—
something that would last, as I was
searching digging grabbing stabbing ferreting
for meaning
but
it was all for naught.
It was all for naught.
But what isn't??
as time's march attacks all things;
& Fate befalls us all.
And only pain fighting entropy* brings.

**Read: status quo, evil, the way of the world, others, anyone, anything... Really, I don't actually like fighting anything. But it seems that many things need to be fought. It's figuring out what's worth it and not that's particularly tricky.*

Entropy is its own demon and I do mean entropy even though I am also mentioning all these other things that cause pain when fighting. Entropy was at the top of my thoughts, because if I didn't make small inroads in reducing the zombie grass every day, if I let the yard go wild, it would become all zombie grass fairly quickly, smothering all other plants it comes in contact with and propagating any way it can: burrowing its ropes deep underground, climbing like a vine, acting like grass: the Loki death plant. But in hindsight, so clear later, I should have been spending that time with my child, using that time to work together on something, talk, help her with homework (patiently), any more lasting way to have spent that time than clawing out grass ropes from the soil, something that one season later looked as if it has never been done...at least those sand mandalas are gone when they are gone and the failure of stopping the thing doesn't meet your eyes the second you step out your door.

Holes

There are so many,
I cannot possibly fill them all.
Some are from alcohol, no doubt.
Some are time.
Chemicals unwittingly inhaled during home projects.
DIY destruction.
Some are not appreciating the moments,
so things got lost as that space is filled with something else.
Maybe I do have vaulted marble halls of storage but I am sadly disorganized.

The insignificance of things, stuff, moments, grains, grime,
and time spent,
doing inane/mundane/insane/hare brained/low gain things.
Find your place on the Animal Farm or head to the Funny Farm.
You pay money and he'll decide if something is wrong with your brain.

This is the last spot with a chunk of white space. During the Kansas Court case, my therapist at the time, a well renowned local therapist for residents of multiple KS counties, who had been involved in many family court cases and worked in various facets of the system for at least three decades, said he had never, ever experienced any parent, anyone, get their rights to their child so ripped away so swiftly, so cleanly, and without any attempts at redress once that decision was made. Drug addict prostitutes have had better court outcomes than I when it came to access to their child, he said. He would talk to his colleagues about my case and they would be astounded at what he would tell them. And never once (over 10 months) did anyone from the court case ever reach out to him for his opinion, to discuss therapy, to work in or on the case. I found my lawyer on the internet and he was worth his weight in maggots, but why didn't he, or anyone contact my therapist? That's one anomaly, that and the fact that I would have to pay a huge sum of money for only one man to present results that only they could see about my suitability to parent my child. My therapist said they'd already decided to put the straightjacket on me, so enjoy the inevitable struggle no matter what you do. Sigh.

Anxiety

never content
always seeking, always striving
she's going the distance, she's going for speed.
Misery is my middle name.
Trapped by my Self, or my idea of others' ideas of my Self,
...my monkey mania matrix mind
can't stop / won't stop.
Striking fear in the hearts of 300+ lb. Men.
So maybe it's true that you had to go,
but that, right now, is not for me to know.
And I will be always tender to you,
your tinder heart needs only alight in the darkest of night,
most other days, it exists in perfect haze,
seeing All, as it's wont to do.
So face this & face that,
my anxiety lessened anew,
as I see long-desired,
kinship and kindness with you.
I never meant harm, I'm just drug-addled, drug-idled, drug-able,
dearest,
caffeine abuse in the DSM-V.
even at my best, I was doomed.

Drugs don’t help

Drug addict.
On drugs right now, in fact.
If I don't have ...
Each day within hours of waking,
My body physiologically revolts.
And basic functions like moving my muscles becomes painful and
beyond trying.
My life sin.
Addicted since 14.
I can only imagine the Hell heroin Brings, if this is my caffeine reality
the daily grind.
Everything is a gateway drug to a brain
And it’s best not to even get started.

And as I edit and go through, I struggle with who and when and what's really good and right as I succumb to each human fallacy. Searching for meaning and…

…good times and great oldies…
…a jingle of truth to the human brain…
…of remembrance and a myth to be found…
…cosmological kindness…

Imagine Me with ALL the Owls

the book has three
but that's nothing.
see them all, little sweetheart,
and try to relax now.
there's a rainbow, then, over it:
nothing. just space.
so see that and sleep now.
peace & wisdom incoming.
the message is dimming from hearing the screaming
so sweet thoughts and peace lovey metaphors
are lost to the meta meat-mega-grinder
of living
as lemmings,
or slaves to our various short-comings,
through wants, by fears,
other disasters we bring…
through incomplete glances and…half taken…

oh good, you're asleep.

These next poems were published as The Velut Luna poems. I haven't changed them since; thank you Poetry Life and Times. (2022)

Dust to dust

We're made of stars
disparate and dissonant.
Day by day
doubt festers,
fenestrations of fear.
And we damn deities,
dredge demons.
Cosmological chaos.
Inherent ideological clashes
birthed from cultural constructs.
Idiomatic onslaught,
shaped by societal mores,
moored by millennia.
Nihil sumus.
herdin' dem cats.

Open

Sometimes I forget to breathe.
Creating a vacuum seal of self.
Presenting that self to the world: an unwilling taciturn tacticality.
The perceived enormity of our individual selves
Lost to the ether.
Lacking time.
Creating space.
Where?

Relativistic Infinity

Effusive energy
Silent fusion
Dominoes without end
A self-made loop
A looped/louped glance,
askance.
Golly gee. Great.
Gutted by greed,
Gouge our evil eyes,
And hollow hearts.
Our irrational ears.
As we fester in finite fallacy.

Outline

where to start?
where to begin?
"We need an outline."
Oh? Oh.
Of my life. Of the complication.
The words swirl in a torrential hurricane inside.
How to order chaos?
"Of course."
It's only a matter of course.
no semicolons. follow the rules.

Velut luna

Spin the wheel
Velut luna

Fortune favors the bold
Tried and true, trite and true.
Therein lies the rub.

Squeezing our infinitesimal selves into the lens
of a long-forgotten dream.

All roads lead you home.
That's as unconditional as it gets.

Changed ex post facto:

Starseed

Particles accelerate
Never losing mass.
Never losing energy.
Cold fusion brilliance,
created in a fog of clarity.
Energy illuminated.
Pounds of stardust
traded for an ounce of perspective.
We all love amusement parks.
Dizzy and delirious,
parked permanently on the ride.

I'm filling the nooks & crannies as I share my voice with you, so I have been going back to fill some space with thoughts as I scroll through. For isn't that what life is: a scrambled account of our fallible memoryweb's timelines of reality? And stories and personas pass down through generations with these tales told through time...so how long until the accounts get blurry, yet sharpened in aspects not actually there? I do want to lose this feeling of this eternal flame. What else in hindsight is needing to be said? There's plenty from my journals that isn't dependent on my current mood or sad stance on the world from my small narrow viewpoint as a girl and woman (for what that matters, but in truth, a lot for how we process and proceed, like it or not) but what life lessons are (t)here? I found essays from college where I interpreted from religious texts that all of us are destined to failure, how, then to proceed-oh god? Thomas Aquinas's concept of soul filtered out as a young person plus all other things I've read and experienced and distilled down into some amorphous understanding of life...More space to write thoughts of continued import as I piece together things I've observed multiple times...the possession of pets is really something odd. You're accountable and responsible for this creature and you love them so much but when they are gone, the sadness too great to have even wanted that snuggly creature: the loss greater than the good parts, wanting in hindsight to not have known that love instead of feeling its loss. That's my personal experience, often (always?), with the pets I've had. And even this concept of "pets," this is largely a US (certainly developed countries at least) cultural phenomenon of ownership and companionship, not worker, the symbiosis and purpose of pets has shifted in this space where we have enough and can impart our opulence on creatures just because we can feed more mouths, so we do. I took in so many strays and then got too involved with too many creatures' struggles. Think of animals as souls and so then balance me inviting in these creatures and although I knew them for a few months, I am devastated at their sickness and I pay hundreds of dollars to try and save them for naught. Bleeding myself for this stranger. Too far. I don't know where that right line is, but that's too far. I've seen in Nepal the wandering cows, wading through the trash and blocking traffic, causing all sorts of havoc and chaos, simply existing as they can't be killed, but they are Souls, so They're here to stay. Enjoy your milk.

"We needn't think of the foibles of anyone's character (are to blame), unless you've started with yourfuckingself and scrutinized every minutia, every second, any minutia, so that blame, couldn't, wouldn't, needn't escape and find rest with any other flame/shame/blame/dame/name. Wouldn't it be nice?" *Psalm Trees on the Beach 12.5*

These three poems were published in Poetry Life & Times, Feb 2023.

:x.

but it's not just that.
permanence and impermanence.
lasting legacy of what and for how long?
stability defined as: x
leaning tower of pisa rights.
perception is reality.
and people leap to their deaths in the virtual world.
I'm standing here firmly in the real world;
but I can't see: where is the line?
& more importantly; who drew it?
how long does it even last in the quicksand?
i kant do that.

webster's

goblin mode, 2022.
ok then...
fragments of my metaverse.
blaming my ennui on my gravity disorder.
Starseedblahblahblah. 5-D suck these Dicks.
i'm genetically predisposed to lighter climes.
it's my woo-niverse.
and the typing cat fervently, feverishly paws out:
the weight of it all, unbearable.

fischschuessel

enjoy the fragmented figments.
flashes of light.
flashbulbs of fame.
reasoning, that recognition fails, fleets, flounders, flops, flippantly flying
from rear-end fenders.
and when does the wordplay stop?
einhalten an alles.
und alle einsteigen.
zack. sagt die stutzstaffel.
protection from what?!

Vision

The grass is always greener, right? So maybe my life *modus operandi* has been never being happy with what I have, where I am, what I'm doing, etc…so I've been searching, always searching. And it's led to fun adventures and lots of experiences. The flip side of that is I've been called a random bad idea generator, as I envision all possible outcomes and scenarios as I fast file flip through my Rolodex of possibilities (my endless wheel of numbers/outcomes) and brainstorm them aloud. Regardless, I think often about what I'd rather be doing, or where else I could be where I'd be more x: fulfilled, purposeful, at peace, rich, whatever it is. Here it is now, my vision for what I want for myself in the future so perhaps I can feel fulfilled and free: own some piece of land where I have dug in the ground so I do not have to pay as much for heating and cooling, have water and solar collection, and a garden. Live very simply and with as little money as possible for myself, trying to grow lots of my food. I will need potatoes; I'll do the research and get some more specifics.

Queue the purple Minion with the underbite.
Sideras, you know the one.

Mirror, mirror.

who's the fairest one of all?
through my looking glass, one side of my face is Quasimodo, so
I'm hoping it's only a metaphorical looking glass.
what is Vision, anyway?
or to capitalize or not, these Nouns?

& reflecting on one's Self is harder than shining the mirror outward,
literally & figuratively (for me at least)–
always looking for faults of others instead of one's own/
shining out provides seeds for gossip & violin victim sonatas
& Stockholm is probably great but

detritus

i got the -itis. (itises/itii)
fasc-, uve-…too many to keep track.
but everything's going, going, gone,
tiny bits
entropy without end,
as the gears grind and the time warps and wares,
dust to dust-itis

The King of Ist frowns.

Universal Truth(s)

we hold these Truths to be self-evident,
that all men are created equal.
Say the slave owners.
Our Founding Fathers.
My country 'tis of...who?
this land of...
so I'm a little leery of these claims.
Grandiose ideas.
I've seen the claw marks in the thickly walled stone holding cells
along the Ghanaian coast--
deep divots in stone
carved by beyond desperate fingers.
where West Africans were stored before the boats came.
And I know I am being lied to
about anything to do with freedom
from anyone.
Smoke and mirrors.

What to do about this? I think of Alexander Hamilton fighting for freedom but was reminded this past weekend that he simply died in a duel with Aaron Burr before his vision was won. Easy come and easy go. & when will it ever be enough? -asks many greats. But we're so parsed into our realities now I can't see true Freedom working for us using anything digital.

This is what failure looks like

but then I remembered I am supposed to talk kindly to myself.
Chin up, look around.
This is what
democracy
choice
republic
&
domination
look like.
nothing is as it seems.
Even then,
event, hen
pigs, chickens, sheep, fish, and cows.
Led to the slaughter,
for you, for me.
& we have blinders on.
We eat our metaphorical selves.
How many doctors will it take…

U.S.o.Re:

tool ply serve ason sult asonate port tighten do done volt view create paint write zoom sume sumptive buke possess peat alistic zone affirm align design vision al cognize colonize

Solomon says

...

I interrupted, for I wasn't listening.
though hope is a broken winged bird that cannot fly,
I said to him.
mine won't perish?
I asked of him.
&
Who put your words on the seat of my petroleum burner and
why?
I can twist your words and put them down myself.
I don't need help.
I declare: I have a silver tongue,
but I will fall
for my quick-temper
Prudence. Temperance.
I am trying to not be impudent and
my temper is...
gone but "can she laugh at the days to come?"*
I'm trying.

**Proverbs 31:25*

The Grand Scheme of Things

the fact that it's all a "scheme" concerns me.
Through MY Looking Glass
subjective.
Ecclesiastes: everything is meaningless
everything is vanity, which is hebrew superlative for the supreme degree
of futility and emptiness.
Everything is relative
ergo, relativistic infinity is reality.
The stars are in my eyes.
Flashes of light,
supernova combustion engines fill my vision space.
Angels. Demons. Spirits. Energy.
Rah-rah-rah-sis-boom-bah.

Life & Times

We're ALWAYS at war.
Societies sat atop mounds of microbes
waiting in the wings.
Some smell rot, others mayo,
some eau'd'toile.
As we're
Puppets with brainstems
helper hosts for
heinous war crimes
upon countless
multiKingdom [insert highest of highs but not infinite] -illions.
Soon,
we'll dig only through the Plasticene,
forced evolution
our devolution
just wait and see.

And seeing in the now too deep, and into the future is hard. Part of my current thinking is about how each of us humans is largely a petri dish for other microbes, largely bacteria. This is with my knowledge of science and microbes and our external and internal biota. Yikes! So depending on how deep that rabbithole goes for our species, humans as mere puppets, an anime zombie sewer person comic book…

And I balance that with the importance of MY consciousness, my conscious actions, my conscience, with science. And as with many things, it's about Balance anyway. (This capitalization of the noun here makes sense, to differentiate it from the verb, anyway…)

King Solomon said

…

I interrupted again.

“I'm just being honest.”

Purgatory

Sit with it. Sit in it. Sit inside it. Sit around it. On it. Above it. Under it. It's f*<king everywhere so you might as well get used to this unintentionally painful, unwitting garden of your own creation.
It feels like a Mactruckheartattack.
But actually, it's a slow degradation, eating me alive from inside out over time
the acid of Existence.
Forced to learn the same lessons over and over again.
“I Object!”
Pound the treatise onto every door.

Lesson

Internal Temperance is the Way.
This is your/my/The Life Work.
Fucking tortoise.

Being One (won) with the Plasticene

thank you, skin, for keeping me healthy.
but everyone thinks you should be more supple.
More elastic.
Tighter,
with less tiny visible holes,
no visible cracks or lines of any sort,
smooth. Unpocked*.
Whisps, whispered ideas, of perfect.
At least I know, deep down, it's so that when our
narrow
shallow
empty
eyes see
we're not reminded of entropy or death or time,
only here, only now, this moment,
comfort.
judge.
and this becomes what we know,
perception of perfection
unrealistic reality.

(* #winning -thank you, again, skin, for keeping microbes from devouring my form: a pox is a pox is a pox and I've just got chicken (and later shingles) to contend with.)

#neverforget the crazy times of SARS-COVID-19 virus madness starting in late 2019 in China but really started spreading worldwide in 2020. If this virus erupted in the Middle Ages what would have happened!? What would the death rate for human have been? Black Plague was ⅓ of the world's population. Fascinating history.
The COVID-19 pandemic so polarizing regarding freedoms and forced vaccination and quarantining more the long take-away than any massive death. And all the unknown unknowns and different people thinking they know this thing or the other…misinformation…disingenuous information…transmogrify the narrative…

Lucky

find a four leaf clover and skip over the rainbow.
Mucus erupts from orifices
but I live.
Fat, even.
I pay for dinosaurs and general primordial sea ooze to keep me warm.
Living large.
How I use my marks of the beast keeps me going.
Strong, even.
Gives me a sense of purpose to
sammeln.
Fuer mich. Fuer dich. Fuer nicht. Fuer alles.
Fuer liebe.
Because that's always a theme,
across cultures, and times, and climes
and we even
personify animals'
biological needs
into love.
Pop songs and poems;
love isn't all you need,
but it is nice.
So I will/should quietly take my luck and be glad my histological
haemotology is going well so far.

Let me tell you, this book will never be perfect. I hope I can remember to take lessons away from the experience. I love the phrase "perfection is the enemy of good" in that maybe you won't even try if you expect perfection. Or in that by wanting to be perfect, you will never be good at anything else because all your time is spent perfecting this (one) other thing. Or in the realization that not everything has to be perfect anyway. But I did rush getting it done initially because I was so excited, & had a goal of being done January 1st (arbitrary). So I did it! But then I began to worry and fret when I realized I wanted a different back cover, one more reflective of me. No instant answer on whether it could happen so lots of anxiety…then I noticed typos in the inner pages! & again I had to ask if I could pause to fix this issue. Yes, thank you, grateful…now, finishing an ASAP submission request after a few days of refining, adding tiny bits, & filling spaces with context. Some of it hasn't even been read more than when it was written is what this means! Cringe! Grimace! But I would rather say things poorly than not at all. I'm available for questions.

Curse

it's part of who we are,
you can't always get what you want.
& that caramel sauce is essential.
So I have a lot and too little,
never enough,
& it's never just right.
Always seeking, always striving.

but I still remember to say thank you.
As I work through it.
I will manage,
and try to *understand* my blessings,
counting them is a bad idea.
Innumerable.
Though sometimes it feels like a big fat zero instead.
At least I still can see with my clouded eyes.

I Voted
proud to pretend I'm ma(s)king change.
My voice matters and the strength of US as a collective...
yadayadayada...
United? What? We stand?
Then why is Everyone sitting?

Thank you, thank you Smith-Mundt Modernization Act of 2012

Wherever you go, the message's the same,
a whole new brand with a whole new name,
we're right, they're wrong,
we're light, they should be gone.
WE kill for justice.
We're on your side.
And I don't want power, oh no, never fear,
but after a taste,
and within a year,
iron fists, shackles, cages.
As puppet strings fetter
us all to the ground,
all evils unknown,
while we writhe all around,
constrained by our blinders,
our limited sight,
enjoying bread and circuses
and what we think is right,
but people are dying
and that shouldn't be so,
as we drop radiation,
democracy in tow.
and each of us helps,
unwitting or no,
as out tax dollars buy
weapons and destruction
and folly as news,
we know what we're told,
we think it's a lot,
as the endless news sates but not giving anything meaningful or true,
what can we as individuals do?

Of course it's not all this bad, right? We're not being spoonfed propaganda, right? We're not at that level of paid programming, right? Especially not with our own dollars from taxes we paid, right? And what we see and hear on the news isn't just an agenda pushed down our throats while many important happenings aren't covered, still occurring but lost in the speeding up of time and the illusion that we'll get all the information if the news never stops when in reality it's even less of all the truth of the matter, right??

Written circa age 20, adapted circa age 40

that might as well have been yesterday. the passing of events in a life are remembered solely as one sees them, and considering many are never seen by others at all; we want to think the past exists as a reality collectively, or is it more truly simply as a skewed illusion of the few, presented at story time, a slighted subconscious dream, haunting individuals in waking and in sleep with the actual facts and scenarios. And the universe of about to be versus decisions once made, after being harped upon, will fade and blur into unrecognizable until the process of decision making in the now which becomes one's life: harp, occur, harp, harp, non-existence, harp, subconsciously rule a realm of dissidence and dissonance inside.

and as much as I enjoy getting to typey-type away my thoughts and feelings to share my subjective reality with others to find some sort of communion with something greater than myself and create something lasting, the futility of it all and the insignificance of self is the tsunami wave that bowls me over, takes my everything, that I guess I did end of crawling out of, and I experience that we all want this for ourselves. I echo that I want this throughout my life in my writing, to be remembered, for what else do we have as individuals. Those guys writing the *Carmina Burana* were just drunks at the local tavern, gambling and losing their fv*k1ng clothes for god's sake(s) and their voices made it out, across generations, across time and place and space. So why not me, too, huh? ...even though it's futile and subjective and self-aggrandizing and ego-laden. And for the modern era, #metoo.

And meanwhile, bars, lines, choruses of song from inside and outside of self sing literal and figurative full orchestral movements of remembrance, lending a concrete basis for every twisting, turning, wriggling, playing dead thought. But the waves reverberate differently over each crevice of space and time, for matter does matter, and the energy translates into entropy. I guess if I am learning anything, it's that fighting entropy is unsustainable, because fighting the inevitable just makes one very tired, but that this idea, this concept, this intangible concept of soul does actually mean something, is something.

Mine isn't "saved," mine is up for grabs, or is it just mine? Does it belong to something beyond me, bigger, greater, better, than my sense of self? And what, even, am I? This universe, this woo-niverse, this fog of our singular and collective reality is something incomprehensible to me and as a result, I have never even once felt grounded or tethered for more than a small period of actual time. And anything that is left, tangible of me, will be subjectively viewed in space, place, and time and misconstrued or misappropriated, misused or disused, translated, transmogrified, transformed, out of context. But maybe nothing does matter, after all, for my smallness, my tiniest dot on the timeline of universal collective reality is just that, dust. Dot, dot, dash.

Teacher

my job title.
Don't be alarmed. I am very conservative at work,
many things I strive to be,
we espouse there
so it keeps me accountable
in a way I might not otherwise have,
so I hold down, tow the line, and
make sure I live by example.
Learning all the way.
So maybe my job is Student, in many ways.
ergo, I like my job.
& I'll take what I'm learning and apply it in all ways,
for there is only One,
One self across all, realms, lands, and places,
so aim to be best at them all.
Queue: Anxiety. Cliffs. Pinnacles. Grand this and that.
Try. Fuck Yoda.

And I know that I have not even been as ground up in the meat grinder nearly as bad as many. There are some who are personally never the cause of their life's grave injustices, playing loud victim sonatas: yawn. I have been incapacitated by my current circumstance of what I see as a grave injustice shaping my current reality. Then there are some that have to sit everyday and go through all the emotions as they sit, jailed souls who did no wrong, held away from life for years, for decades, as we judge and debate their freedom: anger, sadness, loss, regret, bitterness you wouldn't believe. A friend told me, essentially, welcome to the club, tale as old as time if you're a black man in court for anything, injustice in court is nothing new, no thing. And another (wiser–lol, sorry Chris)black man said, upon being asked if there was one crime he could do for the last time and then it would never be able to be done again, he said lie in court, or perjure. This would save many from the meant grinder of 'justice,' certainly. It would have 'saved' you and I from being separated; but as I come to term with these last four years, I think that what if this was for the best? (I kind of have to try to think like this as a tactic so I can cope.) Your assigned high school would have been too big, too competitive; I would revert back to yelling as my parenting tactic. I have learned a lot about patience and grown a lot as a self-reflective person and not just a liver, but did the lesson have to come this tortuous way?! Regardless, I feel ground up by the machine but so are many others.

That's a solid ending, and j/k, Yoda is great, but sometimes trying is all you got. Winging it. but here's more lol 101, or LOL 101, 101 101 (thanks BatangChe font, from .odt software 4.1.12)...

and DARE to be different and DARE to perceive,
what could be/should be
if you DARE to believe.

drugs are bad,
you could never believe!
But take ones that doctors give you sans fail,
for blood-sugar, pains, and paroxysms...
of course it's a farce,
so far-sicle
-wow,
The transmission cut short,
still the intent unerred (unaired):
be careful here, my darling,
the world is weary for all that entreat.

But enjoy, enjoy,
eat drink and be wowed,
for the meddling's severe,
the intent running wild,
but know in heart upon heart upon hearts,
that you truly know best.

And keep, oh, my dear,
semblances taught,
whether fraught with idealism or not,
that love is what does and will always remain,
through thick, through thin,
it's always the same.

And know beyond knowings of knowings of now,
that I love you beyond measure, and how!

And Isabel, irony of all ironies, the kids at school think I'm the most patient teacher. Sigh. I lost sight of who I was and what was important, & how I defined important a moving target. Queue material possessions, suburban cosmology, & stress of ownership: dogs, other pets, two houses, an alcoholic husband; it was a perfect storm for losing sight and even having so much stress I had facial muscle twitches (figured out only in hindsight why.)

Where I am Now

I still don't have any answers, really, about anything; but specifically, four+ years later, why my life was so tumultuously turned upside down; tried in a court of "equity" for something: something that all involved seemed to know, understand, and make decisions about but me. I'm not even sure when, if ever, I will find out what transgressions I actually committed against my child in her mind versus what lies were told to the court, what the reality of the situation was/is. As time warps and wears, and perceptions become memories, especially if they're based on lies, what the reality is/was and what is taken away will not be the same story and truth is garbled, muffled…I expect I'll get some resolve when she's eighteen, in two more years. I hope she'll come running to me as soon as she's 'freed.' I use the word freed, for she hasn't contacted anyone from her 'past' life. Not one person. Which, of course is concerning, given that her father has frequented cult(like?) groups and what not…

So I hope she and I will make up for lost time starting on day 6571. But expectation can be a bitch and hope, while sustaining me right now, might mean I have a big let down coming. I can't think of that, much, yet. Mostly because right now, I still tread water daily in her absence.

Sorting out being a mother, taking care of a human you love more than anything every day, and then never talking to/hearing from her again for many years, receiving no word, no photos...it is a heavy sack to lug around, lots of particles to breathe through, aches that sink deep and then stay. And whether ennui has filled my soul or not during various times in my life, I (still/largely) tried my best as a mother and wasn't angry or bitter in my work. In short, I feel a great loss without end.

And it takes everything I have to sift this out, the lack of truth, the questions (for it's likely evident by now that I like asking and answering questions)...I feel a pressure, a weighted mass in my chest. I feel a blockage in my throat. As my heart breaks over and over and I can't speak my truth and have it matter. I am witnessing physical manifestations of esoteric feelings. Being truly heartbroken sucks.

So feeling care or concern about the selfish and silly ways of Mankind seems wasted, even more than before and I do nothing political, nothing to serve. I will change this, at least serving, volunteering when I can see more clearly outside of my own hell again. Right now I'm largely just in wait and see mode. I don't want to miss anything by not being immediately available and I want to give her all things so I wait patiently and think of her in my every decision. And as I age, I mourn the loss of childhood, both mine and hers. She can say she's seen a lot, (and that is true, but it's all relative), and, I too, had to grow up too fast. I miss that time for myself, and I missed the end of that time to spend with my child.

P.S. to I.L.S.

And making up for this lost time is my justification to do anything for you in your life...like saving all this money, moving to wherever you are, helping you in the ways I can...but I will have to watch out for me being an enabler maybe…overloading and burgeoning problems created by the polar opposite of nothing…I will help you, though, through thick and thin, unconditionally, and do my best, better than I did before. The long and the short of it all is that I want to be around to support you in your endeavours. I want to right any wrongs I've done by you and help you in every way I can.

For life is "just" a series of choices, at least the part we can control. And then, even, the parts that we can't control, that are fated or karmic or luck, how we handle and deal with those, this again is our choice. It's easy to think of the big choices as the ones that shape us, the sliding glass doors of making one decision and the other falling away into nothingness when that trajectory also could have existed. But it's the daily choices and the choices in the daily fog that also shape us. How do we spend our time? Where do we find meaning or search for our daily sustenance? Are we just going through the motions waiting for some other things to come along, some other input, some dopamine hit of a like on Facebook, something, anything to remind us we aren't alone, that we are real and exist and mean something to someone, anyone? So find meaning in self…I am still figuring it all out so that's all I've got so far for wisdom.

But I am getting to the point where I try not to mind about anything such as others' perceptions of me as long as I know I am doing the 'right' thing and I don't need external validation, because as we grow and age, the person we will spend the most time with is ourselves anyway. So these writings are for myself, to have my voice placed down for myself at a minimum, and that being enough. But I like the idea of you, daughter, getting to read my perspective from your age when you were taken and where my mind is the last 4+ years. I like the idea of this providing some help to anyone that might need it, some grounding or anchoring when one doesn't feel any.

And sweet daughter there is plenty more in here not said, both good and bad, as I hear the lies and process what could and could not be true; but, I anticipate that we can work through it all as it comes, and inclusion or not about any mental illness I or you might feel or know, it being mentioned here versus not does not mean it isn't important or attributed. So much of the pain didn't transcribe here, so much of the daily suffering I have felt. Time has at least worn the edges…this creation that I have imagined as I questioned everything and tried to make sense of what was happening to me as lies swarmed and gaslight explosions filled the halls of courts in two states now exists. It isn't perfect, even close, but here is something, tangible, of me, past and present as I tread, float, and flail about in this world. It's for me, but it's also for you as a way to document and process into the future.

Blind

says David (Byrne),
& Jesus saves,
Heals?
the other one says.
when nothing is seen, how to interpret things?
our cult-U-are vision heavy.
through leftovers, siftovers, packages and memes.
imagine just being,
without these things.
then sit there and sit there and sit there more,
and see if you've learned much more than before.
then sit there, stew, muse, and quake,
for you've still got a decent stake,
and you're waiting upon waiting,
by god! each second the longer it takes,
and yet time is so precious,
then isn't it absurd, that one would waste it,
With...

Dot. dot. Dash. Meat-grinder. Hope. Consciousness changers. Game. Marks. (of the beast). Schemes. Cult-u-are. God(s). Mythos. Meta. Ether. Waves and particles. Grappling. Differences. Perception. Reality. Philosophy. Religion. Time. Space. Past. Future. Present. The Unknown. The Knowing. Intentional destruction. Come, go, came, gone. Why.

Come & ride with me on the Fantastic Voyage, ride, ride, slippety-slide
doing what we can just to survive at the
"amusement park for social narcissists"
as we simmer in our "cauldron of self absorption"

I dedicate this:

To my most precious gift from the Universe, my daughter.
I mean that from the bottom of my heart and beyond,
in ways I'm still not sure I understand.
I hope you have known and will always know this in the bottom of your heart.

I found some papers that said your name was to be Sideras Isa Skyfield.
Meaning in Latin “stars that I love better than myself,”
with last name conferring nothing, necessarily.

This little light of mine.
Shine, shine, shine.
Ad Infinitum.
Ad Nauseum.
AD 2023.(Gregorian)
The actual time, space, and place I would like to think is irrelevant.

And I felt so strongly that I could never create a being,
for it would be too much of my heart outside of myself,
and I still think this, which is why (I think, at least)
your existence is special, but there is my ego again, even infiltrating another.

Regardless,

I love you
te amo / Σ ε α γ α π ώ / मुझे तुमसे प्यार है
我愛你
احبك انا / እወድሻለሁ

Watch your thoughts for they become words. Watch your words for they become actions. Watch your actions for they become habits. Watch your habits, for they become your character. And watch your character, for it becomes your destiny!
–Thanks, Margaret Thatcher

& include the idea of any demons you have, these will become you as well–what we think we become. don't let negative thoughts consume you, though it's easy to do.

We all seek to matter.
To mean something.
Myself included.
Thanks, humanity.
& progress. order...
To Infinity and beyond!
Not even to mention the infinite meta magna light beta gamma radio uv
IEEE 802.11b Direct Sequence xG.
You can even have the last word.

entered into the historical record:
AD 2023 Gregorian - way to go US, copycats of all things.
230 French Revolution calendar - WTF France - cancel culture much?
1443-Islamic
2563 Buddh(ist)
2775 Julian-way to fall, Rome, with BS ego infighting
(and, sure the whole calendar changing with Jesus from AD to BC,
a lot to contend with, especially when you wish
instead of Before Christ it was Before Caesar.

(and what's in a year? ... at least we agree on that, right??!)

And what was this book? A birth of Fate?
Manifest Destiny? My version of mindmelt mumbo-jumbo?
LOL 101. IOI 101.

Please check out my social media channels, because, of course.
facebook.com/jessica.skyfield
instagram.com/jpskyfield/
pinterest.com/skyfield/
twitter.com/fieldsky
facebook.com/WEareKansaswater

Also Google my name because you can find some cool stuff if you do.
There is some other stuff but my branding is off.

Here's a (good) snippet for a book review: Skyfield's Condensed Chronology is a scathing tongue-in-cheek, nihilist view of society from someone who hasn't been a willing participant since, really, she could write. However, because her struggle for true goodness is so real, she tries to fix things with their actions but always comes up short. With an unsaved soul and an ego that must constantly be grappled with, the protagonist of this (true) story wants to experience, achieve, and change so much all while largely blind.